A Beautiful Mind, A Beautiful Life

A Beautiful Mind, A Beautiful Life:

The Bubz Guide to Being Unstoppable

LINDY TSANG

SH STYLEHAUL / ADAPTIVE BOOKS

AN IMPRINT OF ADAPTIVE STUDIOS | CULVER CITY, CA

Adaptive Books
3578 Hayden Avenue, Suite 6
Culver City, CA 90232

Visit us on the web at www.adaptivestudios.com and www.stylehaul.com

Library of Congress Cataloging-in-Publication Number: 2017954061
ISBN 978-1-945293-62-7
Ebook ISBN 978-1-945293-56-6

Printed in the United States
Designed by Whitney Manger

10 9 8 7 6 5 4 3 2 1

A Beautiful Mind, A Beautiful Life

Me

S ome of you might know me as Bubz, but most of my friends call me Lindy. These days, some of you might also recognize me as the virtual sister or friend you've watched on YouTube for several years, posting makeup tutorials about products I love using or techniques I've been trying to master. I've been vlogging as BubzBeauty since the early days of YouTube, teaching my subscribers how to put on makeup so they feel beautiful on the outside but, more importantly, to help them feel beautiful on the inside. But for those of you guys who think you know a lot about me, I'm going to take you back in time to a younger me, someone you might not recognize quite as easily, the person I was well before I got up the nerve to post my first video online from my little bedroom at my parents' house in Northern Ireland.

Let me paint you a picture of a much younger Lindy Tsang. Ah, the nineties! It was a sparkly time of body glitter, boy bands, platform shoes, flared jeans, floppy disks, terrible dial-up connections, home telephones, dodgy perms, and did I say body glitter? From what I remember, I was always a pretty awkward kid. I felt different. All the time. And try as I might, I just couldn't fit in with my peers. Even as a child, well before I knew what the word *judgment* meant—I knew how it felt to be judged.

I have a large extended family, and none of us are known for our sensitivity. I have never been a tall person, and my aunts, uncles, and cousins seemed to take pains to point out my tiny stature. Each time they saw me at family gatherings, they would point and laugh, then ask my parents if I was shrinking. Then they would ask me to stand back to back with my cousins to quite literally be measured up against them. I like to think they were genuinely concerned about my health, but regardless of their intentions, my feelings were always crushed by their ridicule. I didn't just look small; I felt small.

But on my own, in the quiet of my safe little bedroom, I could be as big and bold as I wanted. I remember spending most of my childhood under a blanket in my warm cozy bed, writing and drawing my own storybooks. And in my stories? I was the star. My character was cool, confident, and fearless. No quiet, fearful, shy Lindy here. In my stories, I "lived" the life I wanted; I was in charge. I could be whomever I wanted to be. I'll never forget that surge of excitement I would feel each time I opened up a fresh new notepad, ready to be scribbled on. In my room, on those pages, I could be anyone at any time. No comparisons necessary.

My imaginary life, lived out in those pages, continued. In my teen years, instead of a superhero fighting monsters (Spot, my all-powerful talking dog, was my mighty and beloved sidekick), the heroine of my stories was now a global superstar, jetsetting around the world while dating hot, mysterious guys at every stop, a lifestyle about as far from my actual life in the quiet town of Glengormley, Northern Ireland, as you could possibly imagine.

Last week, my husband asked me if I thought I eventually became that character in my book. I thought about it for a while and decided that the answer was no. The girl in my storybook was someone I thought I needed to be. The girl I am today is simply the girl I'm happy to be. I'm still far from perfect (and oddly enough, it comforts me so much to know I'll never be perfect) but honestly, I think I like the real Lindy Tsang more.

I may not be the global superstar of my childhood dreams, but I *have* had the opportunity to travel the world, meet so many awe-inspiring people, and do some pretty amazing things, so I'm doing okay, I guess. But no matter which of my dreams have come true, not much has changed from the awkward little girl I was, because here I am today writing this book for you all. Still awkward, still very short, but let me tell you, life is magnificent. It's a beautiful journey that blesses us with the opportunity to learn, love, and laugh each day. Too many people are missing the magic of life by letting their joy be taken away by fearful thoughts about the past and future. I promise you'll hear me say this again, but it bears repeating: Don't miss this moment. You'll never get it back.

The reason I'm writing this book now is to help remind you how important it is to be present, to take advantage of this moment. It hasn't always been easy for me either. I'd like to help you guys along on your journeys, after being on mine for many years now.

Because I am just like you. I used to be fearful of the future, regretful of the past, and my inner demons (insecurity, bitterness, envy) were eating up my present. I felt lost. In the coming pages, I will tell you stories that might sound familiar, some funnier than others, some a little bit heartbreaking. For most of my childhood, I felt truly ugly, obsessed with my terrible acne, embarrassed about my body, nearly broken by the mean bullies at my high school. I felt as if my family didn't understand me, as I kept choosing a path to please my mother, instead of one that would fulfill my dreams. I found myself in a battle for independence with my mother, while trying to come to terms with a distant relationship with my father. All those difficult and complicated circumstances had led to me living back at home, working part-time as a waitress in my family's Asian restaurant, dreaming of a different life but doing nothing about it. Those inner demons were still controlling me.

But several years ago, I decided to change the way I lived, to change the way I felt about the world around me. Instead of being bitter at all the dead ends I kept bumping into, I decided to take control of my life, and look where it led me! I finally got up the nerve to post my first video on YouTube, and little by little, people started to watch. Then, once my channel started to become more successful, I decided to move from Northern Ireland all the way to Hong Kong to launch my clothing business, despite being terrified of taking such a risk and making such a huge change in my life. But my clothing line ended up being successful, which led me to launch my makeup brush line as well, not to mention sign with a management company that expanded my opportunities to reach people all around the globe.

Now I feel so blessed to be able to travel all over the world to different events and meet with my loyal and amazing Bubscribers, the millions of wonderful people out there who have been supporting me and lifting me up these past few years. With their support, I've also fulfilled my dream of building schools around the world for children with fewer opportunities than I was given. I'm blessed to have a wonderful marriage to my husband, Tim, with one amazing child and another on the way, though family life hasn't come without a fair share of complications.

And it is all because I decided to change. I know it sounds crazy, but you *can* decide to change. And once you come to peace with the world around you, you'll find that inner peace you've been seeking. Once you have found that inner peace, you will be less distracted by your wants, concerns, and desires, and it will be much easier to concentrate on achieving your goals and dreams. I promise.

This book is to show you how to be unstoppable in every area of your life. That's my new dream for you all.

You are going to change your lives for the better, one page at a time. Are you ready?

Follow me . . .

Foreword

by Adam Braun,
Founder of Pencils of Promise, CEO & Co-Founder of MissionU and NY Times Bestselling Author

Lindy Tsang is one of Pencils of Promise's biggest supporters. In less than just two years, with the help of her dedicated community, Lindy has built a total of five PoP schools, bringing quality education to thousands of students around the world. This comes as no surprise from someone who continues to inspire a vast community of over six million people weekly on social media, and has done so for the last ten years.

Whether you've watched one, or all, of her videos, or if you have had the pleasure of meeting her in person, it becomes crystal clear that Lindy is an individual who views the world from a different lens than the rest of us. Lindy holds a special and unique ability to connect with her audience, whether via intricate makeup tutorials or by sharing personal stories about her family. Through her engaging content, she helps millions of people realize that true beauty is about being comfortable in your own skin.

Lindy was first introduced to our organization, Pencils of Promise, through her manager, Kenn, who read my book *The Promise of a Pencil* while traveling through Asia.

After becoming familiar with PoP's work and learning that 250 million children around the world can't read or write, Lindy decided to launch a fundraiser in support of our 2015 Back to School campaign. Within two weeks, she raised enough funds to build two PoP schools in Laos. In January 2016, the PoP team was honored to take Lindy to the field to show her the impact of the two schools she had just built.

Lindy and her husband, Tim, traveled eighteen long hours from their home in Northern Ireland to join the PoP team on the ground in Laos. Upon arrival, they eagerly took on the challenge of participating in our work firsthand. They painted walls and created cement blocks for a new school, witnessed dynamic lessons taught by PoP-trained teachers, attended a school inauguration ceremony, and met thousands of children, parents, and teachers who now have a brighter future because of the collective efforts of the BubzBeauty community.

During her trip, Lindy not only saw the extraordinary impact of an education, she also experienced the true power of her platform and voice. The two schools she built were now changing the lives of children every single day—and will continue to do so for generations to come. By the end of her week-long trip, Lindy fully committed to fund three additional PoP schools by the end of 2016. Soon after this commitment, Lindy launched another monumental campaign, raising over $120,000 for PoP, reaching her goal of funding three more schools! We were blown away.

It's because of generous supporters like Lindy that Pencils of Promise has been able to build over 400 schools in the last eight years, allowing us to bring quality education to over 70,000 students daily.

With the thought of each new school build, I'm brought back to my powerful personal experience breaking ground on our first school in Pha Theung, Laos. This was a day I'll never, ever forget. One particular memory that sticks with me was when I watched the grandmothers of the community carry huge planks of wood into the village. I tried to stop them to avoid them injuring themselves. They absolutely refused to put the planks down, looked me in the eyes and stated, "you don't know how long we've been waiting to carry wood for our grandchildren's first school."

Building that first PoP school in Pha Theung felt like an impossible dream come true. This experience is what ultimately motivated me to truly push forward to grow an organization that would continuously enable that feeling for any other person, family, foundation or business.

Our lives are so often a result of the influential experiences we encounter, and in my case each significant event played a role in creating the trajectory of my life's ambitions. If I could go back to my 17-year-old self, I'd tell him these three pieces of advice:

Surround yourself with people you know will make you a better person. Becoming a young adult comes with countless difficulties and obstacles. You're constantly meeting new, and often very different, kinds of people, as well as trying to fit in to where you think you should belong. It is crucial to become part of a community or make friends with those who will support you, teach you, inspire you, and challenge you to think bigger.

Lindy's work exists to help others realize the sheer beauty in being yourself, doing what you love, and giving back. Every day she uses her platform to encourage others and fosters an incredible online community with followers who choose to be a positive light for one another—and for the world at large.

A goal realized is a goal defined. Set goals for yourself and be ambitious with them—don't limit yourself. Whenever you have a rough day or feel like quitting, these goals will remind you why you started in the first place. They may seem far-fetched as you're writing them down, but all you have to do is make a tiny bit of progress every day. Baby steps. That's all.

"Willing to try. Willing to learn." I love this motto of Lindy's. Her dreams were big, and even if failure was a huge possibility, she persisted. She's now one of the most successful UK-born YouTube stars and beauty experts to date. Her story of perseverance is an inspiration for many. If you believe in yourself, set clear milestones and actively work toward those ambitions, one day you'll surprise yourself.

Being you is more important than being cool. Life so often tempts or challenges you with what may seem like appealing opportunities that you know deep down don't sit right. As a maturing teenager or young adult, more and more often you'll find yourself at a crossroads that requires you to check your moral compass to lead you to your path forward. During these moments, our core values and beliefs become critical checkpoints. These values will guide you in your decision-making process. Always trust your intuition because you know yourself best. Your life is one of radiance—choose to shine brightly and be a beacon onto others.

As a strong mother, bold community leader, and creative taste-maker, Lindy Tsang embodies all these values and much more. Her fierce dedication to her passions, her deep desire to constantly work to make the world a better place, and her fun and optimistic spirit are all attributes that anyone can look up to.

In her decade-long career, Lindy has touched millions of lives and has had countless accomplishments—from viral videos to high-profile magazine features, to fronting ads across buses, billboards, and cinema screens. But her greatest accomplishment of all? Teaching us all that the best way to change the world is by simply choosing to be the best version of yourself first.

This book is a testament to Lindy's character and inspiring life journey.

Table of

Contents

The End

Once, a primary school teacher asked her classroom, "What do you want to be when you grow up?" One child answered, "I want to be a doctor." Another said he wished to be a teacher, another a veterinarian, and another child dreamed of being an astronaut. Then one child stood up proudly and answered, "To be joyful." The teacher looked oddly at the young boy and told him he had misunderstood her question. The little boy smiled, shook his head, and told her, "No, miss. YOU did."

You see, whatever we desire to have, whatever we strive to be, we are all actually wishing for the very same goal. Whether it is:

- A gorgeous, blemish-free face.
- A killer wardrobe that would make Anna Wintour jealous.
- A super metabolism that allows you to eat whatever you want and somehow still have a lean, fit body.
- A successful, blossoming career that would make Sheryl Sandberg proud.
- A dream mansion like the ones you see on MTV's Cribs.

All these different wishes actually come from the same place. We think and hope these things will make us happy. (Whether they will is another question, of course.) But they all have one thing in common: We all just want to be happy. . . .

In today's competitive age, with the never-ending online Armageddon that is social media, in this era of Instagram one-upsmanship, how many of us truly feel good about ourselves? It seems the more we have, the worse we feel. We're more connected than ever, thanks to improved technology, but it feels like we've lost our personal touch. We work so hard trying to fix our supposed "flaws" that we fail to see all of our great strengths and potential. We are more invested in ourselves than ever, but that's not the same as loving yourself. The truth is, *you don't need fixing.* None of us do. What you need to change is your mindset.

This book will equip you with the knowledge you need to build a happier, more fulfilled, and more confident you. You will learn to let go of powerless thoughts, because a powerful mind makes a powerful person.

You owe it to yourself to live that beautiful life you desire. When I say "beautiful life," I don't necessarily mean a worry-free life, living in beautiful homes, and traveling to exotic locations around the world. This book isn't here to teach you how to live a Pinterest life with perfect Instagram filters. Instead, this book will teach you to cherish the imperfect life. With the right attitude, you will learn how to navigate life's blips and bumps much better. A beautiful mind brings a beautiful life.

I'll be here to guide you (and cheer you on in spirit, *woo-hoo!*) but there is one vital thing you must believe: *You* are the one who is truly responsible for your own happiness. You and only you. From this point onward, I'll be here to support and encourage you, but you are going to be your own best friend.

This is the end of you giving away your power. It's time to take the power back for yourself.

Becoming Unstoppable

How do you envision the word *unstoppable*? Maybe you picture a train careening down the tracks. Perhaps you see a powerful raging river flowing down its mighty course. But right now, I want you to picture it as a person. No, it doesn't have to be some sort of wealthy entrepreneur, powerful business executive, or media tycoon. What makes a person unstoppable is much simpler than you might imagine.

An unstoppable person is someone who is not afraid to make mistakes. An unstoppable person radiates confidence because they believe in their abilities. An unstoppable person perseveres by viewing life's obstacles as opportunities to learn and grow. An unstoppable person doesn't just dream the dream; they live the dream. I may stand vertically challenged at 4'11" tall, but I have big dreams. This is what makes me unstoppable.

In this chapter, I will share my journey of how I came to live confidently, boldly, and authentically. Because I wasn't always that way. I used to be my own worst enemy, doubting and questioning everything I did. Does that sound familiar to you? Do you get in your own way? Trust me, you are going to be unstoppable too. I'm so revved up that I can barely contain myself. Can you feel it?

The Power of Self-Confidence

Without a doubt, one of the questions I get asked most frequently is, "Bubz, how can I be more confident?" Ah, the million-dollar question. I'm sorry to tell you that, unfortunately, confidence is not something you figure out once and then, like a magical vaccine, you've got it figured out for life. Many people want to get to a place where they can feel completely self-assured, but this place doesn't exist. Confidence isn't a destination at which you can arrive; it's more like a journey you take every day. And since it is a journey, you must learn how to become a better traveler.

We're all moving along our separate paths, but essentially, we are all traveling along in the same journey of finding ourselves. Isn't that beautiful? Even if your journey has been rough so far, take heart because you are not alone, and it's about to get a whole lot better.

A person with no confidence is like a race car sitting in a garage with an empty fuel tank. It should have the ability to surge at high speeds but, without fuel, it is powerless to pull out of the driveway. What is the point of owning a flashy car when it can't even take you to the places you want to go? Confidence is our fuel. It is what allows us to live bold lives.

Even your personal heroes and the stars you follow religiously on social media experience insecurity and self-doubt from time to time—sometimes a lot. It's completely normal and part of life. As we grow older, we encounter different people and situations, which all will ultimately test our confidence. Believe me, that's a good thing. I believe each time we get pushed down, we get back up stronger.

In life, constant challenges and changes give us the opportunity to learn and love. We're not made to stay in the same spot. Without change, we cannot grow.

When I was in fourth grade, I had the most awesome teacher. Imagine the sweetest little old lady in the world. That was Mrs. Crilly. I loved everything about her, from her cute gray curls to her sweet, grandmotherly scent. Under her thick glasses, her eyes looked huge, which made her even more adorable.

As you might have guessed, I was her class pet. She called me her little dumpling, which I assumed was because of my height, but now that I think about it, that may have been slightly racist since I am Chinese. (Ahh well, no offense taken. I love dumplings.)

After a great year in her cozy, loving classroom, I spent most of the following summer crying my eyes out, knowing I wouldn't be able to return to Mrs. Crilly's fourth-grade classroom. Pssssh, fifth grade. I mean, Mr. Anderson? He'll never be as great as Mrs. Crilly. I was dreading the first day of school.

Guess what? I ended up loving fifth grade. I adored Mr. Anderson, who was kind and funny and always made us laugh. Any sadness I had about leaving Mrs. Crilly behind disappeared. Mr. Anderson was basically a giant ball of sunshine. Change, perhaps, was not so bad after all.

Can you imagine staying in one place all your life just because it feels safe and familiar? Change can feel uncomfortable at the beginning, we may even fear it, but it's exactly what we need to grow. Whether we like it or not, change is part of life. If you're going through a transition in life right now, embrace it. Focus on the things you're about to gain rather than the things you're about to lose.

Life is like riding a bicycle; to keep balance, we must keep moving. Our confidence will grow with each new challenge we face and overcome. Big changes in life, even if they are scary, will always make us stronger and more self-confident. And that self-confidence helps us approach the difficult moments in life with a better attitude and makes our journey along the way more enjoyable. Sometimes we are pedaling uphill, strong and sure. Sometimes we crash and burn on the descent. Despite the dips and blips, the ups and downs in our journey, the key is that we are always moving, learning, and changing.

Self-confidence is the key to being unstoppable. After all, how can you become unstoppable if you don't believe in yourself? If you don't believe in yourself, why should anyone else? Life can feel unfulfilling and lonely when you lack self-confidence. It can hold you back in so many ways—from building lasting relationships, to working hard in your studies, to chasing your dreams. Having self-confidence will open up more opportunities and possibilities for you.

The truth is, we all have extraordinary potential within us. The only thing that keeps us from unlocking it is that other *F* word: *FEAR*. Fear is the greatest enemy of self-confidence. You can't prevent yourself from experiencing fear, but the good news is that you can stop yourself from giving in to it.

If I had let my fears stop me, I would not be where I am today. One thing for sure, I would not be sitting here in my kitchen writing this book. Maybe I would still be doing graphic design work for companies I didn't believe in. Maybe I would've kept my drawing and writing hidden in a box, never letting anyone see the real me. All I know is, thank goodness I overcame my fear of failure and *tried*.

Maybe for some of you, you are afraid of:

- Disappointment
- Rejection
- Getting Hurt
- Change
- The Unknown
- Criticism
- Judgement
- Failure

I once let fear rule my life, starting when I was just a child. I know without a doubt, many of you will be able to relate to my story.

* * *

I've always known that I wasn't the brightest crayon in the box.
That's not me making fun of myself to try to get you guys to say,
"No, no, Lindy, you're super smart!" No, I'm just being honest here.
To be fair, my entire family is ditzy, and I just happen to be known
for being the ditziest one. People are usually uneasy when I touch
their stuff because, more often than not, I end up breaking it. Is care-
lessness a character trait? I don't mean to be careless; things just seem
to happen with me. I trip a lot. Not like Jennifer Lawrence does it,
when somehow it's cute. No, I just fall down all the time, and then,
of course, I get injured a lot. Growing up, knowing how klutzy I was,
my family didn't let me do a lot of stuff. To be fair, after a while, I
may have taken slight advantage of it.

"Don't let Lindy do the dishes because she'll break them. Besides,
they're never truly clean when she does them."

"Don't let Lindy help with the cooking because she'll burn herself.
Or worse, burn down the kitchen."

Perhaps because of this, from an early age, I somehow ended
up believing that I shouldn't trust my abilities. I just accepted that
I was someone who would mess everything up, so I was afraid of
doing almost everything. I'm sure I had a few impressive moments
during my childhood, but to be honest, I can only really remember
the moments I messed up.

Throughout school, I struggled to keep up with my grades. I
would sit in class and somehow, as the teacher droned on, my mind
would drift away. Every day I would come home not having learned

much at all. Year after year, my report cards nearly always had the same comment: *Lindy is a pleasant pupil. However, she must learn to focus more in class.*

My mum would shake her head in frustration and demand to know why I wasn't paying attention. I couldn't answer her. I tried, I really did, but I just couldn't stay focused. But there was one subject where I would always score the highest in the class, so I would always try to make her reread the comments from that teacher. *Art & Design: Lindy is wonderfully gifted in art. She is a natural artist.*

My mum knew I was good at art, and she knew that I loved it. Unfortunately, in my parents' minds, art class wasn't academic; therefore, it just wasn't something worth being proud of. To an Asian parent, as stereotypical as it sounds, the only successful jobs one can aspire to are: doctor, lawyer, or engineer. That's it. You only have three choices, and being good at art wasn't going to help me become any of those things, so it wasn't worth my time or my mother's.

In direct contrast to me was my cousin Laura. She was the epitome of the perfect child. She played the piano, took ballet lessons, and was a straight-*A* student. Every Sunday, we played together while our parents enjoyed a family bonding session over dim sum. Despite growing up with her, I had never realized just how little we had in common, until one day it was made clear to me just how different we were.

One Sunday afternoon, Laura's parents brought her report card with them and passed it around the table. It wasn't just a great report card; it was a perfect report card. My heart sank. Watching these extremely proud parents brag about their child, and watching my mother react with obvious embarrassment, I was so ashamed.

My mother then turned to me and said the following words, which I will never forget: "If you spent less time doodling, maybe you'd be half as smart as your cousin." Ouch . . .

I know in my heart that my mother was speaking harshly to motivate me to do better. But that moment did far more harm than good. She was thinking that I already knew I was good at art, so she should point out other areas I should work harder in. But the words had the opposite effect. They crushed my self-confidence and made me sure I would never be able to live up to Laura's example or my mother's expectations.

The foundation of self-esteem is laid in childhood by the messages we receive from our parents and caregivers. My mom rarely gave me encouragement, which is something I desperately needed, as we all do, to push forward. Growing up, a child knows that it is their parents' responsibility to take care of them. They instinctively trust the people who brought them into the world. A child's sense of worth is almost always attached to their parents, the people who are supposed to love them best.

It's not just that I wasn't always getting the grades my family expected from me. My physical appearance was difficult for me too. Growing up, I always had to wear work clothes made for children much younger than I was. As you already know, I dreaded family outings because the topic of my height was guaranteed to be brought up and ridiculed. However, none of that compares to the disappointment of watching your own mother do nothing about it.

I'm a mother now, and I know I would fight anyone for mocking my son for something he has zero control over. Okay, fine, I probably wouldn't fight them physically, but I would definitely remind my son that it's okay to be different. Maybe my mum didn't want to make a scene, but the memory of her laughing nervously at the teasing, then agreeing with my tormentors, still breaks my heart. It didn't matter what my relatives thought. I just needed my mother to tell me I was fine the way I was.

But it never stopped. *I need to be smarter like cousin Laura. I need to gain weight better like cousin X. I need to play the piano better like cousin Y. I need to be more charming like cousin Z.*

Each time I got compared to someone else, I would be reminded how much I was disappointing my mother. From a young age, it was clear: In order to make up for all my shortcomings, I would have to please her as best as I could in every way possible. I was terrified at the thought of failing her.

Growing up, my siblings and I were mostly taken care of by our wonderful grandparents. We didn't get to see our parents much, as they were working most of the time, so any time I got to spend with my mother was precious to me. In my mind, my mother was (and still is) the most beautiful woman. She was always nicely dressed, and her hair was beautifully styled every day. I looked up to her so much; I wanted to *be* her. Because I had to fight three other siblings for her attention, I never had much quality time with her, so it made me even more desperate for her affection. As long as she accepted me, I felt like I could accept myself. So I was always trying, trying so hard to get her to accept me. I was obsessed with pleasing her.

You might be wondering what my dad's opinions were. The truth is, I don't have too many memories of my father from my childhood. He was totally dedicated to us, but he just wasn't a big part of our lives. As a child, I was hurt that he was never around, but now that I'm older, I understand that it was only because he was incredibly busy trying to make a living for his family. In order to give us an above-average life, he sacrificed time with us. As a typical Asian father, he may not be the best at expressing his love for us, but we know the love is there.

You may wonder if I still hold any resentment toward my mother now. The answer is no. I carried the burden of our difficult relationship inside my heart for many of my adult years. I kept asking myself, "Why couldn't she have behaved this way instead?"

One day, it hit me hard that I needed to stop idealizing how my mother *should've* been. She wasn't. And I can't change that. So why obsess now about what she *didn't* do? My mother had me when she was very young, and like all mothers, she made mistakes along the way.

Once I stopped being angry about all the mistakes she made as a mother, I started to look at her as a human being, a vulnerable woman with plenty of fears of her own. This change in mindset helped me feel compassion for her. I started to understand her better. It wasn't that she was trying to be the way she was; she just didn't know how to be any other way.

I realized that she wasn't just hard on me. She was even harder on herself. Because *her* parents had nitpicked everything she had done, she ended up developing the same bad habit. Parents are not infallible.

Once I started to have more compassion for her, I stopped focusing on what she isn't and focused on what she is. Besides, who am I to judge? I am nowhere near perfect myself. Heck, I can't even count all the times I have accidently banged my son's head on the door frame (oops) or lost my temper after a long day. My mum would take a bullet for me, this I know. I could've ended up with far worse parents. Besides, I can't push all the blame on her, because I fed into her behavior too. I am responsible for my happiness, not hers. And that conclusion, finally, brought me a lot of peace.

Despite all of the rough patches, I ended up doing extremely well in my studies. Even though I still struggled to absorb information in school, I would go home every day to rewrite passages of my textbooks over and over until the information was etched into my memory. The entire house was covered in Post-it notes to help me memorize better. I was absolutely swamped with coursework during weekdays, but I still made time to help out at my parents' restaurant on the weekends.

By now, Mum was extremely proud of me. I became known as the obedient child. I was happy because alongside all my studies, I also got to do my favorite thing in the world—paint. Art & Design was one of the subjects I studied for my A-level exams, and not for one single moment did it ever feel like work. For me, it was an escape. Each time I picked up my paintbrush, all my problems disappeared as I immersed myself in a different world.

Then it was time to start applying to universities. My art teacher, Mrs. Hall, strongly encouraged me to study fine art. She even personally made a list of good universities for me. I didn't know what to say to her. Would this be something my mother would be happy about? It wasn't even a question. Why would she want to fund me for "doodling"? Looking back, my mother might have hesitated, but now I believe she would've let me go through with it. But I decided that she would say no. I was too afraid to even consider the option. I doubted if I would ever be able to find a "real job" afterward. I gave in to fear.

I ended up applying for a course that was at least somewhat related to my interest in painting. I decided to study Graphic Design & Packaging. Surely that would make me more employable, right? But I would get to remain creative too . . . right?

I was wrong. I soon found out I couldn't care less about designing shampoo bottles and soup packaging. I thrive on creating art with paintbrushes and pencils, not tablets and trackballs. So I really struggled. Halfway into my first year, I knew I had made the wrong choice enrolling in that course. But I hated the idea of becoming a university dropout. I had dealt with the hassle of moving all the way to Sheffield, England from Northern Ireland. I couldn't just move back, could I?

I told myself that I needed to give this course a chance. By my second year, I hated it even more, but by then I had decided that it was too late to drop out. What got me through all that misery? I allowed myself a blissful fifteen minutes of free time each day to watch YouTube makeup tutorials. I know that you've all heard of YouTube, but back when I was in university, it was only just starting to become a thing.

Even though I hated my course, I pushed on, telling myself it wouldn't be long until it was all over. I don't know how, but I ended up surprising myself by graduating with a BA honors degree. But even so, stepping off that campus was one of the most freeing moments of my life. Goodbye, miserable life. Hello, freedom. Mum was happy about me graduating, and I was too, until I realized it was time to enter the real world. Now I have to look for a job . . . ?

To be fair, it's not like I didn't know this day would come. I was just too afraid to contemplate the reality that was heading my way at breakneck speed. Don't we all want to avoid the difficult, scary questions? Instead of truly envisioning and planning my future, I chose to stick my head in the sand, for as long as I could. If I didn't think about it, I wouldn't have to deal with it. I procrastinated out of fear, and, just like when you overspend on a credit card, I was left with a big fee to pay in the end.

Here's the thing about graphic design, my "chosen" field. It is arguably one of the most popular majors out there for creative types. I'm guessing a lot of other fellow artistic students also decided to opt for the more "employable" route and also chose this field. The issue was, when I was finishing university, the United Kingdom was going through a huge economic crisis, and there were just not enough jobs to cater to the huge number of graphic design graduates. To find employment, you really needed to make sure your portfolio stood out from the rest, or that you at least had some sort of experience working in the design field. But the field was so crowded and competitive that even in order to get an internship, you needed to have prior experience. Okay, so now I needed experience to get experience? I was doomed.

I had chosen a field I wasn't passionate about in order to be employable, but then it turned out to be one of the most difficult paths I could have chosen to find a job! I may have pushed myself just far enough to get my degree, but with my glaring lack of interest, it was not enough for me to stand out from my peers who happened to be truly passionate about and talented in graphic design.

"Lindy, your sketches are beautiful, but do you have any digital work you can show us? Perhaps a website concept design? Also, do you have any experience at all in this field? What makes you want to be a graphic designer?"

Hmm. Those were great questions. Perhaps the fact that I *didn't* want to be a graphic designer was the reason I didn't perform well in my interviews. I had to admit that it was time to rethink my life plans.

A bit crushed, I returned to Northern Ireland to live with my parents. I was dreading seeing my family and having to answer all their questions. Surprisingly, though, my mum wasn't upset at all. It seemed as if doing well in university was enough for her. Coming back also meant that I could help out in the family restaurant full-time, so this was a case of win-win for her. She had basked in the moment of glory when I graduated, but that was the extent of it. Now what she really wanted was a trustworthy family member to help out at the restaurant.

I was feeling utterly hopeless and bleak about my future, so I agreed to work there full-time while I looked for employment. This situation was no one's fault but my own. I had made these choices and would have to live with them.

The restaurant wasn't the fanciest or the most modern, but it was cozy and warm. My father built it inside a cottage and brought nature inside by placing lots of greenery around the dining area so it resembled a greenhouse indoors. Most of our customers were regulars who had been coming to us for several years. I realized that many would come not only for the good food but for the good banter as well. It may seem a bit crazy, but I knew all about our regular customers' professions, family members, likes, dislikes, and favorite pastimes.

Since I was the boss's daughter, everyone who worked there was required to be nice to me, though unfortunately that didn't include the customers. As a family member, I definitely got the worst end when it came to complaints. Usually most customers were pretty understanding, but every once in a while, I would encounter really mean ones who just seemed to be out to get free stuff.

"This is unacceptable. What do you mean this is a Chinese restaurant, and you don't serve Chicken Masala and naan bread? I will NEVER come back here again, and you can be sure I will share the terrible service to everyone on my Facebook page!!!"

We were a Thai and Chinese restaurant, so of course we didn't sell Indian food there, but this lady clearly just wanted to throw a fit. I remained calm and gave her a steady smile, but that was one of those moments where I wondered if possibly I wasn't cut out to be a waitress. But mostly I have great memories from my time working there. Each night, I did my thing and that was it; I didn't need to worry about anything else. It was easy and comfortable, but something was always missing. This wasn't where I was meant to be for the rest of my life, and I knew it.

Since my job didn't start until 5:00 p.m., I had most of my afternoons free. My fifteen minutes of happiness per day on YouTube had helped me get through my final year in university, and now that I was back home, my love for it didn't wane. The enjoyment and entertainment I found on YouTube was also the highlight of my mundane life in quiet Whiteabbey, Northern Ireland. I was still living at home, but now that I was receiving a weekly wage from the restaurant, I was, for the first time, able to afford makeup. I was finally able to experiment. (A lot!) I quickly became immersed in this new world of beauty and makeup, and I felt like I had found excitement and passion again in my life.

At the time, there were only a handful of beauty vloggers (we're talking about ten years ago). On one sunny afternoon, I still can't explain why, I plucked the courage to film my first video. Thinking back on it now, I want to giggle. That first upload was nowhere near professional standard, but I honestly just wanted to share whatever I was learning with the world. In a lot of ways, I was quite lonely being back in Northern Ireland. Although technically I was "home," all my friends and my boyfriend were still back in Sheffield, so I felt isolated from everyone I cared about. I badly needed companionship at that strange time in my life, so I think that's why I decided to reach out to the world on YouTube.

I could be wrong, but I believe my very first YouTube video was a product review on a foundation I was obsessed with at the time. I filmed and edited the whole thing using my MacBook. To be a serious YouTuber these days, you have to invest in a great quality camera, lighting setup, microphone system, and editing software.

Back then, I just needed to use my built-in webcam from my laptop, and I was good to go.

I remember how nervous I was, uploading that first video. I canceled and re-uploaded it several times, because I kept having second thoughts. The uploading process took forever; with our awful connection speed back home, it took at least three hours to upload a short, low-resolution video. Then the video went live. I had taken my first step out of my comfort bubble into the big wide world. That was the day my life changed forever.

Mind you, I didn't exactly set the YouTube world on fire. If I'm not wrong, it took me about half a year to gain one hundred subscribers. But I never gave up; those one hundred subscribers were everything to me. They frequently commented on my videos, and I even got to know them pretty well individually. It was such a special time, back when I got to interact with each and every subscriber—I truly miss that level of contact, and even friendship, with the people who supported me way back in the beginning.

At the time, I didn't tell people about my new hobby. I felt that as long as I kept it a secret, I would have zero pressure on me. I was afraid of how others would perceive me, since back then, YouTube wasn't well known. Instead, I felt safety and companionship in the presence of my subscribers, who were all anonymous and many miles away.

When I first started out on YouTube, I was probably uploading videos once or twice a week. Back then, it was more normal to upload once a week (these days, people seem to upload daily, if not more often). But even if I was only posting once or twice a week, I was often filming several more times.

Since I had the morning and afternoon free, I would spend part of my day filming, then after my shift at work, I would come home to edit my videos and reply to all the comments and emails I received. I spent my days collecting inspiration through books and magazines and making my scrapbooks.

Skincare has always been a core interest for me, probably due to all my skin problems as a teenager, so I spent a lot of time experimenting in the kitchen, testing as many DIY beauty treatments as I could.

I was learning so much every day, and I just felt so motivated. I woke up excited every morning, anticipating the day ahead with a smile on my face. The experimenting was so much FUN!! I started to play with colors that were well outside my comfort zone. I was amazed how badass I felt just by applying a darker lipstick. Different looks put me in different moods, and different makeup styles started to feel like different outfits to me.

I could spend hours experimenting with different makeup and hairstyles, not just on myself but also on my family and friends. I was kept quite busy, as my subscribers were always feeding my inspiration through requests. They kept me up to date with whatever was on trend. My subscribers are still the ones who keep me in the loop, and this is one of the many reasons they are my inspiration.

One day, a few months after I started posting videos, one of my videos ended up being featured, which meant it made the front page of YouTube. Not long after that, it was featured again, each time exposing more and more viewers to my channel. At this point, all my numbers started to grow: both the number of views and the number of subscribers. When I reached ten thousand subscribers, about a year and a half after I posted my first video, YouTube made me what they call a "partner." It was a huge celebratory moment for me. This meant I was now able to monetize my videos to make an income from YouTube.

Honestly, at the time I didn't even think much about this factor. I was just so excited to finally be able to have a pretty banner above my channel page. I viewed the money I might generate from my videos as pocket money for makeup. My future was suddenly looking brighter.

Despite everything that was going on, I still had barely mentioned my secret hobby to anyone. Some of my closest friends were aware of what I was doing, but my family didn't really understand the extent of what I was involved with. Only my boyfriend knew at the time, but even still, I kept everything vague. It was something that was my very own, and I felt safer not having to explain to everyone what I was working on.

One day, when I was driving us both to work, my mum and I got into a heated argument. She had noticed I was spending more and more time in front of my computer, but when I tried to explain to her about my newfound passion and possible new career path, she just couldn't really understand what I was doing or why. To her, the idea of having a career based on YouTube was both nonsensical and of course, a joke.

"You're wasting your time," she said harshly. I slammed on the brakes and turned to look at her, furious.

"You don't have any faith in me. You're looking down on me, aren't you?" I questioned, my voice shaking with anger. She jerked back, and I could see the shock and confusion in her eyes. This was the first time her little girl had ever talked back to her. There was a short pause as she stared at the road in front of us.

"Honestly, I'm just waiting for you to fail," she said with a chuckle, without looking at me. Maybe she chuckled to break up the tension. Maybe she really thought everything was just a joke. Either way, I was crushed.

At that point, I was twenty-one years old. I had spent so many years taking in her criticism and saying absolutely nothing. For the first time in my life, I was starting to feel confident about something again, and I wasn't about to let her take that away from me. Not anymore.

"You know what, Mum? I'm going to show you," I responded, smiling defiantly and looking her straight in the eyes. She laughed but didn't respond. Then we both dropped the subject. We didn't speak for the rest of that day at work, but by the next day, we had put it behind us. But I have never, ever forgotten her words. For the next year, the idea of proving her wrong fueled me.

Looking back on it now, I don't blame my mother for ridiculing my focus on YouTube. Of course she had trouble understanding the idea that you could make a living from making videos, as did many of my friends. Back then, that whole online vlogging world was unknown to so many people, and my mother just didn't understand. I also wonder if I should be a little bit grateful for her harsh words. They certainly lit a fire under me that pushed me to succeed on my terms, no matter what.

By always comparing me (unfavorably, for the most part) to everyone else, my mother made me afraid she would not love me unless I did things her way. But if I'm honest with myself, I can't put all the blame on her. I embedded that fear into myself. I know she would've loved me regardless.

I had lived my entire life making choices based on my perception of my mother's happiness. But after all that time, I was starting to understand that chasing her expectations would be a never-ending cycle; that bar would be set higher and higher each time. I would end up emotionally and physically deflated whenever I tried to fit into her definition of success. Trying to keep her happy left me unhappy with my life choices. I finally realized that I would not be able to fulfill my destiny if I was too busy trying to live my life for others. It was time to let go of her goals for me and start to make some of my own.

- Fear stopped me from believing my mother would love me regardless.
- Fear caused me to shrink back and hide.
- Fear stopped me from doing the very thing I loved the most.
- Fear stopped me from doing the right thing for myself and my future.
- Fear stopped me from accepting myself.
- Fear stopped me from being myself.

But then, I was tired of being in the back seat. I was ready to become the driver. I didn't know exactly where I would end up, but I was prepared to take the wheel.

Not long after our argument in the car, as my mum was doing the dishes one afternoon, I confronted her.

"Mum . . . this YouTube thing? It's not going to be a phase. I know what I'm doing. I really appreciate you giving me the opportunity to work at the restaurant, but I also want you to know that I most likely will have to leave in the near future. I know you had high hopes of passing the business on to Ricky and me, but the restaurant has always been dad's dream, not mine. It's just not what I want to do. I'm sorry. . . ."

My mother turned away from the sink slowly and looked at me, not saying a word. I clenched my fists, expecting the worst but unwilling to back down.

"I'm going to have to start doing things my way now, Mum. Even if you don't understand, that's okay. Even if it's not important to you, understand that it is to me. Believe in me, okay? I hope you will support me."

When I finished speaking, she took a deep breath and turned back to her dishes.

"Okay, daughter. You're a big girl now. Mummy trusts you."

Those words were like music to my ears. With tears in my eyes, I gave her a gigantic hug. I had just taken my first step toward taking control of my life.

It wasn't easy, but I was so proud I had finally told her exactly what I thought. Confrontation can be extremely difficult, but sometimes it's exactly what is necessary if we want other people to stop controlling our lives. The thought of confronting my mother was terrifying; I had spent years trying to do the exact opposite. But once I finally got up my courage to stand up to her? It didn't feel so bad at all. In fact, it felt completely liberating.

"The only thing we have to fear is fear itself." - Franklin D. Roosevelt

Soon enough, my YouTube ad revenue started to outearn my weekly salary from the restaurant. It felt incredibly satisfying to know that my income was entirely my doing, that I didn't need any help from family or friends. I had been intending to save up for makeup school, but life apparently had other plans for me.

One day, I was out picking up supplies for the restaurant, daydreaming about a different life, as usual. As I parked the car, I suddenly had an amazing idea. What if I designed my own T-shirts? I already had a built-in audience; perhaps I could finally put my knowledge of graphic design to use, while still getting to be creative in a way I enjoy. I was so excited about the idea, I walked into work and immediately started doodling different T-shirt designs on the back of a greaseproof chip bag in the restaurant's takeaway kitchen.

Everything happened quite quickly after that, because the timing ended up being perfect. My boyfriend, Tim, who was still living in Sheffield, where we had been at university together, had just graduated. He was looking for a job, and he became very excited about my idea and agreed to design an e-commerce website for me.

I carefully selected a few different styles of shirts, then bulk ordered them online. I bought a heat press, for making your own T-shirts, on eBay for £130. Then I searched for the best-quality transfer paper I could find. This sounds absolutely ridiculous, but at the time, the cheapest and best way to handle this situation would be to print my designs out on an inkjet printer, then hand cut them out and transfer them using a heat press. It sounds rudimentary and labor intensive, and indeed it was, but this was how my merchandise line began. I named the brand "Bubbi," after my online presence name. I borrowed a sewing machine from my best friend and began to practice how to hem the neckline. Looking back, I did a terrible job at it at the beginning, but at least I was willing to try and willing to learn.

The world says no to you in a thousand ways:

- "You're too young."
- "You're too old."
- "It will never work."
- "You don't have any experience."
- "I don't think it's a good idea."

In my case, the question was always: "What if nobody buys your stuff?" My mother asked me this a number of times, out of concern. And I can't say I never contemplated that outcome. The investment in all those supplies and equipment was a good few months' worth of my pay, but it's not like I invested every dime I had. I decided if it all failed, at least I would know that I tried, and I would have no regrets. Fueled with the excitement of continuing to take control of my life, I had a good gut feeling inside.

I hand-pressed every single shirt and packaged them all by myself. Tim and I were nervous, but we took a collective deep breath, and the website went live.

I could not believe it. Every time we refreshed the page, the numbers of shirts being sold skyrocketed. They were literally flying off the shelves. The shirts I spent weeks making were sold within minutes. In less than one hour, we had to take down the buying option. I was going to have to press a *lot* more shirts.

It was the most satisfying feeling, shipping those orders all over the world. I was so happy to spread positivity to all my amazing subscribers. But the excitement soon faded when I realized that this little side business was way too much for me to handle alone. My hands became blistered and sore from the burns I obtained from using the heat press. I would often feel faint from the fumes after working for too long.

One morning, I woke up to find Annie, my best friend, waiting at the front door, holding a little suitcase in her hand. She showed up in my time of desperate need to help me as much as she could. In the midst of those hectic nights, even my mother joined to help into the early hours of the morning. As chaotic as things were, I was truly happy because I felt so touched by everybody's support.

I knew it was impossible to sustain our little business working like crazy people into the wee hours every night, so we started to look into the possibility of getting the shirts manufactured somewhere instead. Tim and I traveled all over Northern Ireland searching for manufacturers, but the prices were far too high. It would mean we would barely be able to make a profit after taking away the cost of manufacturing and shipping.

"We could look farther away . . . like in Hong Kong?" Tim suggested.

"You're kidding," I responded in disbelief. Hong Kong? That sounded so distant, complicated, and kind of scary to me. "You mean, move there??"

"I'm serious," he said. "My aunt knows someone who runs a factory in Tsuen Wan. Maybe we could operate our business there." Tim clearly wasn't joking, not at all.

"I don't know. I can't just leave Mum and Dad's restaurant like this. . . ."

"Think about it, Lindy. You keep saying you want to make your own choices in life. Now's your chance."

He was right but, to be honest, I was too scared. I felt happy and comfortable in my home, I had a car I loved—how could I leave my beloved Chad, my Mini Cooper? I loved being able to see my family every day. My grandmother depends on my weekly drives to get her grocery shopping done. How could I just pack up and leave?

"But, Tim, we don't know anybody in Hong Kong! I've lived my entire life in the UK." I couldn't wrap my head around this idea. Hopping to the other side of the globe, into a different time zone, to start a business just seemed too scary. The fear paralyzed me.

In the end, Tim went to visit the manufacturer in Hong Kong by himself. He was serious about that idea, far more so than me, and to his credit, he saw a way to make the business work for us as a couple, while also making sure the business could grow and succeed. We kept in touch through MSN Messenger for the entire three weeks he was away. One night, I logged on to see that he had left me a one-line message on my screen.

"Lindy, pack your bags. We're going to Hong Kong."

It was happening. Tim, during his trip, managed to find a manufacturer in Hong Kong that would make our existing designs for a decent price. Mr. Yeung, the guy in charge, would normally not work with such a small business. However, he was somehow intrigued by our story and wanted to give us a chance. Tim was thrilled.

The downside? He needed a minimum order from us, and the number he gave us was *much* higher than our usual stock. We would need a whole lot of cash just to pay off our first batch. Would we even make enough to break even? Unlike the last time, when we weren't spending every last dime we had, this was a true risk. Not only would we have to spend almost all our savings, we would also need enough spending money to survive in Hong Kong, and we'd have no immediate family there to help us if we got into trouble. I suddenly pictured Tim and me begging on a Hong Kong street corner for change.

Sometimes, when you're afraid, you just have to embrace it. Do it afraid! The unknown scared me. The uncertainty of our future scared me. How was I supposed to know if things would work out over in Hong Kong? A voice inside reminded me, "You will never know." Nobody knows how tomorrow will unfold.

Furthermore, were things always wonderful where I was? Was everything going perfectly in the current version of our lives? Not necessarily, but it was certainly easy for us. So we decided it was time to leave our comfort zone. Yes, things were comfortable and safe at home in the UK, but we were ready for a change. If everything fell apart, at least we would know that we had tried, and we wouldn't have any regrets not taking a chance on ourselves.

Within a few weeks, we flew to Hong Kong and gave ourselves a year to make it work. We spent most of our hard-earned money on paying for that first round of stock and on our one-way flights from Northern Ireland.

The day I stepped onto the train to leave for the airport, I looked back to see my best friend, Annie, with tears streaming down her face and her nose running like a faucet. As she waved goodbye, she told me something I will always remember: "You go take over the world, Bubzbeauty." (She really said this!) I nodded to her as I (barely) fought back my own tears. But that moment cemented something inside of me. I decided, right then and there, I was going to be unstoppable.

Everything wasn't quite as scary as we had initially imagined, thank goodness. Since my father lives in Hong Kong half of the year due to work commitments, he offered to let us stay in one of his apartments rent free, which relieved us of a huge extra financial burden. We would be staying in Sha Tau Kok, out in the middle of nowhere in the New Territories, but at least it would be quiet, spacious, and, most importantly, free. We were truly grateful.

Our trial of one year in Hong Kong ended up being six amazing years. If it hadn't been for the birth of our son, at which point we decided to move back to Belfast to be closer to family, we would have stayed even longer. With the success generated from the shirts, we invested the profits into creating our makeup artistry brush line. Now that we have a family, we no longer have the time to manage our product lines. Instead, I collaborate with companies I trust; I do all the designing, and they handle the rest.

I've since gone on to design my range of bracelets and recently launched my signature eye shadow palette. The best part is, I'm still designing every single day, and I don't intend to stop anytime soon. We are so lucky to be able to live comfortably as a result of all this hard work and good luck, but I can tell you that what makes me truly feel rich is simply being able to learn and create every single day. Money equals wealth, yes. But doing something that gives you meaning—that is what leads to a rich life.

Where did all this so-called success begin? It wasn't when I posted my first video. I wasn't when I started making more money than my waitressing gig paid. It wasn't when I pressed my first shirt. It wasn't even when we took a huge chance and moved to Hong Kong. It started back when I decided that I was in charge of my life. For so many years before that, I held myself back and tried to make excuses for my unfulfilling life. You may have rolled your eyes when you read how much of an insufferable suck-up I was to my mother. I don't blame you at all, because even I didn't like myself back then. I knew I was a coward. The day I let myself be *me* was the day I freed myself to all the possibilities out there.

*   *   *

Strengths over Weaknesses

"Everybody is a genius. But if you judge a fish by its ability to climb a tree, it will live its whole life believing that it is stupid."

Confident people tend to concentrate on their strengths rather than their weaknesses. Confident people are aware of their weaknesses but choose not to let those weaknesses define them.

In terms of things I'm confident about, I'm a little all over the place. On a scale of one to ten, when it comes to my sense of direction, for example, I'll give myself a three. I am terrible at math, and I always have been, so I would at most give myself a five. But this score might be a result of my poor math, so it probably should be way lower.

However, I would grade myself a comfortable eight at communication. If I invested more time and effort perfecting that particular quality, I could possibly be a nine or even a ten. Maybe you're a great listener, storyteller, painter, writer, or even have a fantastic sense of humor. The point is, we can all be a ten at something.

Bill Gates is without a doubt one of the most successful leaders in the world today. With that being said, I bet he has weaknesses too. Would he be even more successful if he worked on his weaknesses? I'd say so. However, it might mean he would not have focused as much time and effort on his strengths to do all the incredible things he has achieved today.

I am not a good public speaker. I stress out about saying the right words in the right moment, so I would not do well in front of a large crowd. As a result, I stutter and blabber for the sake of saying *something* without making any sense. But I have been told that I have a knack for engaging with my audience, and whenever I have the chance to inspire someone, I find my fear of public speaking falls away.

For the longest time, I've felt most comfortable in my little bubble behind my camera in my home. Some people are made for lights, camera, and action, but not me. Perhaps if I put more effort into perfecting my public-speaking skills, I might one day be able to lead a powerful presentation. However, I can also choose to focus on finding more ways to engage with others and possibly inspire them, say, in the form of a book. After all, unlike public speaking, writing a book allows me all the time in the world to reflect on my thoughts and how to say what I want to say.

But let me tell you, writing a book is one of the scariest things I've ever done. Before I started working on this book, I spent a good month or two procrastinating. I had barely lifted a pen since high school. I could easily express myself in the form of a video, but would I be able to say what I want in writing, instead of out loud? That is the question, a question a publisher once asked me that I failed to answer, a question that paralyzed me. I put a lot of pressure upon myself because frankly, I didn't want to look stupid. The fear of failure, of embarrassing myself, stopped me from being able to put a single word down on paper.

Then a friend said these words to me: "Lindy, you don't have to worry about trying to sound smart or having perfect grammar. What makes your book great will be *you*." That made a lot of sense. I am not an amazing writer, but my passion to reach out and inspire people will help me get through it. Instead of letting my weaknesses hold me back, I will focus on my strengths. A confident person does not dwell on their weaknesses. As long as my book sounds like *me*, who cares if it's perfect?

Don't Compare

You already know that growing up, I struggled with the feeling that I was always being compared (usually unfavorably) with everyone around me. I used to blame it on having so many amazing cousins, who all seemed smarter than me, taller than me, and more beautiful than me. But as I got older, and a little bit wiser, what I came to realize was that even if my family hadn't made me feel inferior, I would have subconsciously done it to myself.

Don't we all do this? We look at the people around us and decide that they are more fit, or more attractive, or smarter, or more successful than we are. We do it all the time, and it's because of how we feel about ourselves, not about how we feel about other people. Since I was never truly content with myself, I just sulked around and watched as the world seemed to one-up me all the time.

"Comparison is the thief of joy." -Theodore Roosevelt

Comparisons are unhealthy and unnecessary. I know this now, but it took me years to realize that I was doing it to *myself.* I can't help but sigh, thinking back to all the years I've wasted being bitter and feeling I wasn't worthy.

We're all meant to be different from one another, right down to our unique fingerprints. Yet I find all us humans doing all sorts of things in order to fit in, to become more like everyone else. The question is: How can we succeed at being ourselves when we are so busy trying to be someone else?

I know people who compare themselves so much to others that they refuse to even try anymore.

"What's the point? I'll never be as good as _____," they'll complain.

Well, guess what. When you say that, the game is already over. You've set yourself up for failure before you've even begun. We create our own futures. If you doubt your abilities, you will end up limiting your possibilities. It doesn't really matter how you stack up against that person sitting next to you. You just have to be good enough for yourself.

As we all have discovered by now, social media is both a blessing and a curse. I love being able to keep up with my family and friends through social media; even when I'm thousands of miles away, I get to tune in to what they are up to. But far too often, we are all guilty of comparing our behind the scenes to other people's Facebook or Instagram highlight reels. It somehow seems to happen more often when we are having a bad day; we end up comparing our worst with someone else's best.

I'm as guilty of this as anyone else. I have a friend I've looked up to for many years. I have never told her this before, but Leah (not her real name!) was and will always be a huge role model in my life. Not only is Leah beautiful and smart, she is also incredibly talented at almost everything. Her accomplishments have always amazed me, but they also remind me of everything I'm not. As proud of her achievements as I was, I couldn't help but compare our lives. I'd have trouble taking my eyes off my mobile phone screen as I scrolled through her pictures. How could someone be so beautiful and successful at such a young age? She had achieved and experienced so much that it made my brain hurt.

Even her boyfriend was the face of perfection; on a bad day, he could still pass for an Abercrombie & Fitch model. (Can you imagine how beautiful their children would be?? Because I have, more than once . . .) All their photos were always posed in the most artistic and romantic way, nothing cheesy or cliché, just a gorgeous couple straight out of a big-budget romantic movie.

This is a true story: Once, I was in my bathroom, scrolling through her feed. There she was in a picture, sitting on top of a magnificent cliff celebrating yet another spectacular moment in her life, while I was sitting on a toilet seat in my messy bathroom under a laundry rack where my husband's boxer briefs were drying. My life felt uneventful and boring in contrast to hers.

I turned off my phone, exited the bathroom, and walked into my living room, only to find my oh-so-charming husband, with no pants on, sprawled across the sofa, picking his nose.

"McDonald's or KFC for lunch?" he asked with a goofy smile. I threw a cushion at him.

"What happened to us? Remember when you shaved and wore pants?"

Fast-forward to a couple years ago, when I crossed paths with Leah again. I don't get to see her very much, as she often travels for work, so I was excited to catch up with her when she was in town for a work event. Unlike the rest of us, who would be there all day, she was only scheduled to be around for a few hours before jetting off again.

When I got there, a bit late and flustered, there she was, on time and looking runway ready as usual. I gave her a huge hug. Her hair was artfully styled in big loose curls, her outfit was perfectly put together, and even with very little makeup on, she looked as polished as ever.

It had been a long time since we had last caught up, but I noticed right away that something was different about her. She looked exactly the same, but the normal sparkle in her eyes was missing. On this day, her eyes were completely flat. I had been keeping up with her life on social media, and I had been excited to ask about all her future plans. But instead of bringing all that up, I felt the urge to ask her gently if she was okay. We had been friends for a long time, although we weren't incredibly close. She gave me a weak smile.

"Yeah . . . I guess," she answered carefully. Usually I wouldn't press for more from anyone but my best friends, but my gut instinct was telling me to try again.

"Are you sure?" I asked. She took a deep breath, and I got the sense she was about to spill, but before she could answer, she was whisked away by an acquaintance of hers.

It wasn't until an hour or so later when I got to see her sitting by herself again that the truth started to come out. I sat quietly, smiling but not speaking, hoping to give her time and space to say what she wanted to say.

"How's your family?" Leah asked, breaking our silence.

I smiled and gave her a quick update on my son, who was at that point several months old, crawling and getting into all sorts of trouble. I showed her a few pictures on my phone and felt relieved to see her smile.

"He is precious. I'm glad you guys are happy, Lindy. It's good to be happy." I don't know why something inside me pushed me again to ask what she meant. Was she not happy herself?

She paused for a long time, then looked calmly at me.

"Not for a while," she said with a blank smile. How could she look so nonchalant while sharing such heartbreaking news? I gave her a comforting smile, but I was speechless for a few moments. I wanted to hug her and tell her everything would be okay, but something stopped me from doing so.

Thinking back, I think it was because I had always imagined her to be invincible. I had believed she lived the perfect life, yet here she was, sitting in front of me, in real life, completely raw and vulnerable. I didn't know how to respond to her at first because I felt like she was far too worldly to listen to my advice. Maybe all she needed was a sounding board. So instead of talking, I sat and listened. This time, I looked deeper into her eyes and realized how worn-out she looked. Mind you, she didn't look physically tired, but her eyes were missing that spark.

All this time I had merely admired (and envied) her life from afar. Like being in a tour group at the White House, I got to see the public rooms of the building, but I never got to explore behind the locked doors. Leah had always dreamed of making an impact on the world, and she did. Unfortunately, along the way, she became lost in the chaos of her success. She struggled to adapt to all the changes. Like a child that had to grow up overnight, her eyes opened up to a whole new, very complicated world. While she was conquering the business world like a champion, her personal life had suffered.

Now that she was suddenly such a "useful" contact, she frequently felt used when meeting new people. She found that she couldn't tell if someone was being a genuine friend or simply trying to network. Her heart hardened, and she suddenly didn't know how and who to trust anymore. Leah became a workaholic and had no time for herself or her family and friends. She was running on a few hours of sleep a day. To prevent herself from being taken further advantage of, she built walls around herself. She did this for protection, but what she failed to realize was, the walls would also keep the happiness out.

I had gushed about Leah's exciting life for over half a decade to all my friends. Successful and beautiful, it seemed as if she could have anything in the world she wanted. Yet here she was telling me she wanted *my* life. For a woman that had always had so much focus and direction in her career, she was lost in life.

On social media, we all know that people only show what they want others to see. You can never know someone's full story because you are seeing the public version of their life, not their private one. Leah's life is the perfect example. On the surface, everything looked impeccable, but underneath all the likes and glamorous pictures (even the ones with #nofilter), she had to admit she was empty inside.

When you spend money on temporary pleasures, you will only get temporary happiness. You get what you pay for. Just look at all the celebrities out there who end up falling to drugs and alcohol and entering rehab. If being successful and beautiful is the key to happiness, why are the happiest people in the world sometimes the ones that have the least? Your life may seem mundane and ordinary to you, but there are many people out there who would love to have a less complicated life.

Not long after I spent some time with Leah, she ended up taking a much-deserved break from her work. I'm incredibly proud of her for all her accomplishments, but I'm even more proud of her for allowing herself time to rest.

We are all built differently, so of course we should all be living different lives. We're not meant to share the same destiny, so why constantly compare ourselves to the people around us? If you think about it, the comparisons add no meaning or fulfillment to our lives; they just distract us from it. Fact: The grass is *never actually greener* on the other side.

It is easy to believe someone's life is perfect when you just look at the pictures. There could be affairs, domestic violence, and betrayal behind a carefully posed family portrait. There could be self-hatred, depression, and anxiety behind a stunning selfie. There could be emptiness and uncertainty behind a graduation portrait. What people project to the outside world rarely shares the struggles within.

We all have our strengths and weaknesses, our perks and quirks, our highs and lows, our triumphs and struggles. We will have them all at different points of our lives. Is it fair to compare?

When I was about ten years old, when we were still living in Glengormley, my parents sat us kids down and announced we were moving into a newer and bigger house. We were all excited, but I was especially thrilled because I had spent my entire childhood sharing a bedroom with my older sister. She was entering her teen years and starting to get pretty hard to handle. I was getting tired of being kicked out of my own bedroom so she could have "space for her thoughts."

"Daddy, will I finally be able to have my own bedroom?" I asked my father.

"Of course," he answered, smiling.

"Will we have a big garden to play in?"

"Of course," he answered again.

"Will it be bigger than Uncle Steve's house?"

I saw his expression change from a smile into a disapproving frown, and I sat back, wondering what I had said that was so wrong.

"Lindy, the only time you should look at someone else's bowl is to see if they have enough. Do you understand?" he firmly rebuked me.

What's funny is that I was actually eating a bowl of rice at the time. I was so confused by his response. I looked around the table, and everybody seemed to have enough rice in their bowl. What did he mean? I nodded awkwardly but deep inside, I thought he had gone crazy. For many years, I didn't understand his words. Now I realize what a good lesson it was. A more contemporary version of this parable was made famous by another very wise man, the comedian Louis C.K.

The only time you look in your neighbor's bowl is to make sure that they have enough. You don't look in your neighbor's bowl to see if you have as much as them." -Louis C.K

What my dad was trying to tell me was that there is more to life than having it all. Life is not about having the best of everything, but rather making the best out of everything. You cannot experience true fulfillment unless you learn to serve others. Instead of looking around, we should look within. Life isn't about what we have but rather what we give.

Create a Better You

Let's be honest: In life, someone will always be better. Don't let that stop you from *being the best for yourself.* You do you, my friend. You have to remember that just because someone is "prettier," it doesn't mean you are ugly. Just because someone is "smarter" doesn't mean you are stupid. Just because someone is more "successful" doesn't mean you are a failure. Who says you have to be the absolute best in everything?

How do you deal when someone is "better" than you? Even if you are secretly envious on the inside, be honest and open about their success. Acknowledge their accomplishment; better yet, congratulate them. Far too many people have too much pride to admit when others are better. They let the jealousy fester inside themselves, and eventually they give in and are cruel toward others to make themselves appear bigger. Who are they kidding? You cannot lie to yourself, so why not just choose to be truthful, inside and outside? Remember, it doesn't mean you are being fake; it simply means you are being honest. Jealousy is a type of fear, a fear of comparison. And you need to face your fears to overcome them.

Choose not to compare. Instead, let the success of others inspire and motivate you. Learn from their values, attributes, and qualities to make a better you.

If you have a role model, or someone you truly admire, instead of trying to "be" them, think instead about what their life values are. For example, let me tell you about my cousin and one of my best friends, Yannie. She exudes a positive aura everywhere she goes. Everyone loves being around Yannie, and even when she isn't in the room, people sing her praises whenever her name is brought up. I have found I always feel at peace around her. Yannie is not only incredibly genuine but also patient. You know how sometimes you will ask someone how his or her day is just to be polite? Well, she isn't just being polite. If she asks you how your day was, she will sit and listen intently to your response with all her heart. Even if you talk about something dull, like trying to find a suitable neutral paint color for the storage room, she will really listen, sympathize, and pour her heart into trying to help you find the best shade of beige.

Yannie inspires me in many ways to be a better listener and a better friend. I often talk too much and forget how to be still. I suspect sometimes people feel stressed when talking to me, because mid-sentence, they can see me already aching to reply. Why am I always in a hurry to answer anyway? Is what I'm saying more important? Obviously not.

Yannie is not super wealthy. She is not running a Fortune 500 company. She is not volunteering in dangerous places or saving lives on a daily basis. But she always knows how to make everyone feel significant, which to me, makes her more "successful" than almost anyone I know. She has a quiet kindness that not a lot of people have, and it makes her one of a kind. But I try not to be envious of Yannie. Instead, I try to develop more patience to emulate the things I love about her.

Be your Own Star

What I love about what I do for a living is the fact that it's been nine wonderful years since I started posting on YouTube, and I am still learning every single day. I thrive whenever I'm inspired. Sometimes I worry that the day I stop doing YouTube will be the day I stop learning. These days, I come across fellow YouTuber friends who are extremely hardworking and determined. Many times, I get a little nervous about how lazy I appear in comparison.

To be perfectly honest, I have sometimes felt slightly embarrassed in the past about being a beauty vlogger. Some of my fellow YouTuber friends are ridiculously talented. Some have angelic voices. Some are body doubles for famous football players. Others are amazing scriptwriters. Some are excellent producers. Others are great actors.

And me? What do I do? I film myself putting on my makeup. Sometimes I think, well, gosh, anyone can do what I do. I would love to give myself extra credit for my brilliant video editing, but after almost a decade on YouTube, I still use iMovie to edit my videos. (Believe me, many fellow creators have cringed at that response.) People call me a YouTube OG (original gangster), a term used for individuals who have been on YouTube for a while. But even after all this time, I am still an amateur at editing my videos.

A few years ago, I was part of FanFest Singapore, a huge event across Asia where you get to watch your favorite YouTube creators perform onstage. I was completely honored by the invitation, and I jumped at the chance. I can't believe it never even really occurred to me that, seeing as how this was a performance show, I would actually need to *perform* on stage. I mean, what?? Comedians can do a live stand-up routine. Artists can sing. Rappers can rap. Musicians can play their instruments. What am heck am I going to do? Can you imagine watching someone do their makeup onstage? Just how painfully dull does that sound?

In the end, I did a collaboration with the MC and Singaporean comedian, Dee Kosh. Together, we had a laugh on stage by doing a blindfolded makeup challenge. The audience had a great giggle, but I couldn't help but feel like my performance was far less worthy than the others. After my segment, my friend Jason Chen, who is an amazing singer, was up next. I watched him from backstage throwing T-shirts into the crowd. Girls were screaming, in awe of his beautiful voice and his charm, and I couldn't help but think, "Man, I wish I had an actual talent. Why did Jason have to perform right after me?"

After the event ended, I was sitting in the greenroom, still envisioning different scenarios in my head. What if I had done an acrobatic performance onstage? How cool would that be? I can barely even touch my toes, but maybe I could learn how to do splits. I was starting to get serious with my absurd daydream of teaching myself how to become some sort of gymnast so I'd be ready for the next performance event, when I noticed a group of girls staring at me from outside the greenroom's glass doors. They were all jumping and waving frantically. I looked behind me to see if they were looking for anyone in particular. Then one girl pointed her finger at me. They were looking for me? I wasn't supposed to let anyone in, but I got up from my chair and started to make my way toward them. I noticed one girl in the group was crying. I started to worry, thinking something must be wrong, as I swung open the door to greet them.

Each of the girls greeted me with a big, warm hug, but the petite girl who had been crying was hysterical by this point. She just kept apologizing, hiding her face behind her hands. I was panicking because I didn't have a tissue on hand, wondering what I could do to help this poor girl.

"Anybody have any tissues?" I called out.

Someone finally produced some tissues, and by that point, I had figured out that she was actually crying for me! When I meet people who become so overwhelmed that they start to cry, I feel incredibly guilty, because I just can't help but feel unworthy of those precious tears. I hugged the girl and tried to make her laugh, telling her how unfair it was that she was still this cute even when crying. I felt reassured to see her smile again. To change the topic, I then asked the girls if they had enjoyed the show.

"YES!" they replied in unison. "Especially your part!" one added. Wow. I felt so unworthy; these girls were giving me so much positive energy.

"No way. You must be joking. I'm nothing compared to all those comedians and singers." I shook my head, laughing. "You know what? It only occurred to me tonight just how little talent I actually have." I swear I wasn't intending to seek attention or sympathy, but I wanted these sweet girls to understand I was really just like them, that I didn't feel worthy of their admiration.

"But you touch people, Bubz," the petite one responded.

"Excuse me?" I touch people?

"Yes," she smiled, as she blinked through her tears. "You touch people's hearts," she said softly, one hand on her chest.

I beamed at her in response. What an incredibly kind thing for her to say. Instead of being proud of myself for having the courage to get onstage in front of all those people, not something that comes naturally to me, I had been criticizing myself all day about my lack of talent. Yes, I can't sing, nor can I do stand-up. My video-editing skills are decidedly amateur. I'm not the most creative when it comes to my content, and there are many more people out there with far better makeup skills.

However, according to this young girl, I can touch people's hearts. To me, it was so simple but so big at the same time. At the end of the day, what do I want most people to get from my videos? Great makeup tips? No, that's not it. The thing I wish for most is for my viewers to feel self-love and self-acceptance. As silly as it sounds, maybe my talent IS my personality? What better gift can you give someone than making them feel more beautiful on the inside?

Before the girls left, they gave me a bag full of letters and gifts. I spent the rest of my evening reading their letters with tears running down my face. I was beyond touched by their heartfelt words. I had no idea my videos could have such an impact on their lives. I keep every letter my subscribers have ever sent me; each time I question myself, I read these letters to remind myself that I am the way I am for a reason.

The great thing about YouTube is that there is something out there for everyone. We all come in different sizes and skin colors, and we all have different interests, talents, and missions. We all cater to the myriad different personalities out there. Just like in this world, we are all made to be different too. Why? Because we all need one another. We can't all be doctors in this world. We need teachers, cleaners, chefs, security guards, waitresses, project managers, supervisors, authors, artists, designers, engineers, illustrators, painters, builders, vets, garbage collectors, and nurses.

We all have limitations. I'll never be a famous opera singer or an Olympic gold medalist, but if I can inspire people to be unstoppable in their lives, that is more than enough for me. Instead of focusing time and energy comparing our shortcomings with other people's lives, we should celebrate our unique identities.

Some of you look up to YouTube stars; some look up to Hollywood stars. And that's okay, as long as you're looking up to them as inspiration about how to better yourself, and not with envy at how much better they are than you. But never forget—we are all the stars of our own lives, shining brightly with our own light.

Optimistic Attitude

I had an interesting thought as I was starting to write this book, something I'd never thought about before. I just figured out that I have never met a confident and fulfilled person who is not optimistic. If you think about it, that makes sense because a pessimistic attitude gets you nowhere. While an optimistic attitude broadens your horizons to bring positivity and hope, pessimism limits possibilities and fills you with doubt and negativity. When you let your mood control your actions, just how far do you think you can get?

Pessimistic attitude:

- *"It will never work ..."*

Optimistic attitude:

- *"I could give it a try."*

Not too long ago, I designed and released an eye shadow palette, and the eye shadow names are inspired by twelve qualities I think everyone should live by for a beautiful life. As you can guess, one eye shadow is named "Optimistic."

Optimism is powerful; it means you rise above your circumstances. It makes you *unstoppable*. A pessimistic person can easily feel defined and defeated by what happens "to" them. An optimistic person acknowledges they are never defined by their circumstances; an optimist takes responsibility for what happens in their life. They live with the attitude that a chapter of a storybook is never more powerful than its author.

Over fifteen years ago, before my beloved grandfather passed away, our family house got robbed. Thankfully, my parents were at work when it happened, and my grandmother, siblings, and I were over forty miles away, in our cousin's home. Unfortunately, my poor grandfather was home alone at the time when four or five men broke into the premises. They ganged up on him, battered his head with a stick, took off his glasses and stamped on them, before tying him up in a corner. Can you imagine how terrified he must have felt? They took everything. Precious jewelry that had been passed on in my family for generations was snatched away. Even my parent's wedding rings were taken.

When we returned the next day to the aftermath, our perfect family home was unrecognizable. Suddenly our little safe haven didn't feel so secure to us anymore. We were all so distraught.

My poor grandfather did not own an extra pair of glasses, so he used a Band-Aid to tape the broken bridge pieces back together until he could replace them. To my great surprise, as we all walked around the house, moping at the chaos, he was smiling to himself. I was shocked. Was he concussed or something?

"Grandpa, have you gone mad?" I asked incredulously.

He scooped me into his lap. I curled up in his arms, studying the wonky frames on his bruised face, and I could feel my heart break in half. How could anybody beat up a sweet little old man?

"How could you be smiling, Grandad?" I asked him through tears. "When I'm older, I promise I will buy you a new pair of glasses."

The words he said next will be engraved on my heart forever.

"Lindy, they may have taken away my glasses, but they didn't take away my perspective. Your gramps can always choose to smile," he said, soothing me as he wiped away my tears.

My grandfather was a man of few words, but he chose those words carefully. And he always said the right thing. I was too young to understand at the time, but now I do. Yes, the thieves may have broken his eyeglasses, but they did not take away his ability to see things clearly. The burglars took away physical things that meant a lot to my family, but we still had the most important thing of all: We had one another. Things will always be things; by definition, they always can be replaced. My grandfather was happy to be alive with his family, something that isn't so easily replaced.

Sadly, my grandfather passed away a few years later after a short battle with lung cancer, and I never actually fulfilled my promise of buying him a new set of glasses. It breaks my heart as I write this, but at least I know that my grandfather, a man with a great outlook, didn't need glasses to help him "see clearly."

Several years later, while I was studying in Sheffield for university, our student home got broken into while we were sleeping. My housemates were furious. Not only did they take the Playstation, but also our bread? When it happened again a week later, that time they took our ham too. (We joked that they must have been trying to make a sandwich.)

I actually have a laugh thinking back to it now. The feeling of intrusion is awful, but I could still choose to be thankful. I could choose empathy. I'm thankful that I didn't need to steal. I can't always change my circumstances, but I can change the way I look at them.

My grandfather's words, and his optimism in the face of such bleakness, constantly remind me that things will always just be things. They can easily be taken away and that's okay. My worth is not counted in material possessions. That night in university, as I lay on my student-housing bed, instead of counting the things the burglars took, believe it or not, I fell asleep counting my blessings.

It's easy to play the victim card by blaming others. From my experience, it's the people who blame the world for their problems who are most unfulfilled and unproductive.

Maybe you have been mistreated, perhaps you suffer from poor health, maybe you come from a broken family, or maybe you don't look the way you'd like to. I understand that for many of us, we have a very real and valid reason to feel angry or sad. It's normal. After all, these emotions are natural, right? However, you must remember not to let these emotions control you, as they will only hold you back from being happy.

Here is one thing you need to remind yourself of again and again, even if it isn't always the most pleasant thing to hear: You, and only you, are responsible for your happiness. The world does not owe you a pain-free life. You cannot depend on others for happiness either.

People are human, after all, and as humans, we all make mistakes. Very often, it's the ones that love you the most that hurt you the most, right? But blaming others doesn't end up making them feel worse—it only makes *you* feel worse.

True joy has to come from within. A best friend encourages, supports, and understands. Always choose to be your own best friend, rather than an enemy. Choose power over pity. Choose victory over being a victim.

Don't just dream it, do it.

These days, I see the word "dream" everywhere I go. I think we are all obsessed with the idea of dreaming.

- Dream BIG!
- Chase your dreams.
- Never stop dreaming.
- Follow your dreams.
- A dream is a wish your heart makes.
- KEEP DREAMING.
- Dream some more, damn it.

I read the pretty, calligraphed dream-related quotes on diaries, journals, wall prints, sweaters, and even underwear. And okay, I have to admit, I buy them too.

Why are we so obsessed with dreams? Good dreams are lovely, really. Maybe you feel like you're floating on fluffy white clouds. Or you're in a beautiful mellow place with sunshine and butterflies all around you. That's nice, but do you want to know how to actually make dreams come true? By waking up.

Some people are so busy looking into the sky, they dream their lives away. Meanwhile, others have woken up to actually make things happen through dedication and hard work. The dreamers are left behind wishing their lives had turned out differently.

- "I wish I were as successful as she is."
- "I wish I got to travel the world like he does."
- "I wish I were as hardworking as she is."

Honey, I'm sorry to break it to you, but those people didn't get there by wishing it. They got there by getting their butts in gear and dedicating time and effort to their goals.

I used to be an avid dreamer myself. You remember those storybooks from my younger years. Whatever I couldn't be in reality, I would make it happen in those books. My heroine, coincidentally named "Lindy," could make all my dreams come true. It felt delicious to imagine those wonderful things, but in the end, they did not happen.

After my years of solitary dreaming, I went on to become the bluffing type of dreamer. This was a long phase in my life. I would spend all my time talking about my dreams to my friends and family: what I wanted to do, where I wanted to go. I would rant and rave about how I would soon leave my dull, uneventful life behind for a spontaneous new adventure. I would spend hours and hours pinning stuff on Pinterest and liking inspirational quotes and photos on Facebook. But was I actually making anything happen? Again, no.

Next up: my procrastinating-dreamer phase! This was slightly more productive than my all-talk stage, because I spent a lot of time making timetables and mood boards. It all sounds great, doesn't it? But I was too busy making everything look pretty. I was so busy planning what I was going to do that I ended up not doing anything at all.

You don't get a prize for dreaming, even if you're really good at it. You can dream, you can wish, but nothing matters until you act to make your dreams a reality.

If you don't have a dream, know that it's more than okay. What's more important is that you have the strong mental attitude of being willing to try and learn. You may not know it yet, but every single one of us has a gift, knack, or talent that gives us joy and can lead us to a path of fulfillment. If you are still trying to figure out what your special talent is, why not sit down and do a little self-analysis? It sounds a bit scary, but I promise you it's a lot simpler than you think.

Go sit somewhere quiet. Take a piece of paper and just start to write down a list of activities you enjoy. What is something you can you spend hours and hours doing? What do you find yourself most drawn to? What are you best at? What are you often complimented for? Go ahead and ask your family and friends to get their opinions too. If you are struggling to come up with a list, my advice is for you to go out there and try more things.

What's the point of trying something you're not even interested in? Well, how will you know until you try? You, my friend, cannot predict the future. This is what makes life so fascinating. My dad spent decades without a hobby until one day, he was dragged out to play golf by one of his best friends. He had spent years and years being sure that golf was a boring sport made for snobs. Now, ten years later, he eats, sleeps, and breathes golf. These days, it's rare for me to see my dad without a golf club in his hand. Sometimes, in order to find the right path, you must attempt several different paths beforehand. Life is about learning, after all. You have plenty more to give than you could ever imagine.

After the birth of our son, I used to complain about not having enough time anymore. I thought I knew how it felt to be busy until I had an infant permanently attached to me. This little baby was completely dependent on me for survival. Then it occurred to me that it's not that I don't have time. I have the exact same number of hours in my day as everyone else.

It's how you use that time and how you prioritize your tasks. I love being a mother to my child, but it's not easy being a full-time mother with a full-time work schedule. At moments, I do struggle to keep balance, but I've learned to work at a pace that suits me best. If anything, I am accomplishing even more now. I'm not saying you must burn yourself out. Instead, I'm saying that it's possible to manage your time differently. I used to wake up late and work late into the night. Now I realize how much more productive one can be if you rise early. Like I said before, in order to pursue something big, you may have to make sacrifices along the way. Who said getting where you want to be is going to be easy? You need to ask yourself if it's worth the fight.

If you are doing a job that doesn't fulfill you, take time on your days off to study a part-time course on something that interests you. If you feel like your workplace isn't offering you enough experience, know you don't have to feel enslaved to it. Think about the long run instead. My sister took a big step back in her career by leaving an unfulfilling full-time job for a low-paying internship at L'Occitane. To make things even more complicated, she had to move from Belfast to London for it. Can you imagine how financially stressed she must have been?

But everything was worth it in the end. In her previous job, she was making boring spreadsheets for a pharmaceutical company; she had no room for creativity. But at L'Occitane, they allowed her to take charge of a number of creative projects. The experience she gained in the company was priceless. They adored her so much that she even managed to extend her internship. After completing her time there, she was able to use that internship as a huge stepping stone to find a job she really loves, also in London. April's "setback" ended up bringing her miles ahead in the end. Now April gets to live and work in one of the most exciting cities in the world, while doing a job she loves.

I know full well it's not easy to trust that things will always work out, especially when you're faced with difficult decisions. After I graduated university and was struggling to find employment, I remember making that list in my bedroom I mentioned to you before. Here's what it looked like:

What I like doing:
- *Painting*
- *Storytelling*
- *Designing*
- *Crafts*
- *Communicating*
- *Makeup*
- *Being a dork*

I looked at my list and put my head down on my desk in frustration. How on earth could I make a living doing these things? Nonetheless, when I turned to making YouTube videos, it was purely out of enjoyment of a new hobby. I didn't intend to make a career out of it, and I certainly didn't plan to become a YouTube persona. I just thought I should try something different. Then, as it turned out, the more I opened myself up to trying new experiences, the more I wanted to keep learning. The more I was inspired, the more I wanted to inspire. The more I stepped out of my comfort bubble, the more I hoped I could achieve.

I discovered my life motto during this crazy ride:

Be willing to learn, and be willing to try.

Having tried is always better than never having tried at all. A few years ago, when I wanted to launch my clothing line, I didn't wait for an opportunity to come my way. Instead of waiting for somebody to hire me to design for them, I took the initiative by doing some research and sketching out my designs. More recently, when I decided I'd like to write a book, I didn't wait for a publisher to come and magically discover me in my living room. I searched high and low for the right team to work with. When there is a will, there is a way.

If you want to write a book, start writing right now. My friend, and one of my subscribers, Bella Forest, lived and breathed writing. As a kind, friendly gesture, she sent me her first book, called *A Shade of Vampire*. The book was written and published entirely on her own. After she wrote it, she made it available on Amazon, then crossed her fingers. Since then, over six million copies have been sold, and it has received over eighteen thousand five-star reviews. Isn't that amazing? I could not be more proud of my friend.

If you want to travel the world, start saving. Dedicate yourself to a savings plan. Spend less by using your money wisely. You may know my brother as RikehTube on YouTube. He used to prattle on endlessly about how he wanted to see more of the world. Can you blame him? He had spent most of his life in tiny Northern Ireland. Now don't get me wrong, my country is absolutely beautiful, but I understood where he was coming from. I told you all about our family restaurant, right? From the beginning, it was always destined for my younger brother to take over the business. All three sisters had grown up helping out in the restaurant, but we each ended up taking our own career paths. My family was depending on Ricky.

For Ricky's entire life, he had always been told that he would inherit the business. It's not that he was ungrateful; it's just that he felt that there was so much more for him to see and give before settling down for the rest of his life in the same town in which he had grown up. The family restaurant will always be there. Before he could commit to it, he wanted to go out and take on the world himself.

As much as I wanted to support my brother, I will admit I didn't pay a whole lot of attention to his dreams. Because for most of his life, Ricky would often take the easy way out. Even if he became passionate about an idea, he would lose interest easily. My brother usually didn't finish things he started, at least not without a lot of help. I knew he would never be able to save up for traveling if he continued to spend his money faster than he could save. Every payday, he would instantly splurge on expensive shoes and crazy nights out. My mother would often joke that he was usually the last person to enter work and the first one to leave. For this reason, I don't think any of us ever took his "traveling plans" seriously.

But one day, he proved us all wrong. Mum was surprised to see Ricky start arriving to work early and leaving late. Rather than messing around, he was suddenly giving 100 percent at work. He stopped going out so much and even adopted a healthier lifestyle. He was dedicated and actually nearly silent for most of the year. Instead of using all his time bluffing, instead he put his energy into action.

And today? My little brother is spreading his wings to fly to Australia to find employment. By getting serious about work, he managed to save enough spending money to hopefully last him for a year. He has spent most of his life in a safe, protected bubble; now he is going out into the big world to discover it for himself. As worried as I am for Ricky, I know this will be amazing for him. There are so many unknowns—he doesn't know how things will unfold—but in his mind, he has nothing to lose.

My family jokingly made bets on whether he would even last six months, never mind a year, but we all truly wish him the best. But it doesn't matter what we think—this is his adventure. He is doing something not a lot of people would have the courage to do, and he is going to soak up as much life experience as possible while he's there. I am incredibly proud that he will never need to ponder "what if." He, and he alone, made his dreams happen.

Oh, remember that "silly" list I made in my bedroom? Turns out that I do each and every one of those things, every single day, in my job now. Seemed ridiculous at the time, but my list pointed me in the right direction, and now look where I am: doing the things that I love for a living. Don't underestimate how powerful it can be to take a moment to figure out what you really love.

And once you've figured out the things you really love, it's time for you to take control: of your life, of your negative thoughts, of your future.

Bubz's Rules

- You cannot live your life based on other people's expectations. It doesn't matter how good you are at pretending; you can fool the world, but you can't fool yourself. Don't be afraid of being you. You need to know deep in your heart who you are or people will try to tell you who to be. Be more afraid of living a phony life than of disappointing others.

- If you've realized you've taken the wrong path, it's okay. It's never too late to start down a new one. It takes great courage to start again. Mistakes can be a good thing because they give us an opportunity to try again and do better.

- Sometimes, seemingly bad luck ends up with things working out for the best. When one door closes, as they always say, another one usually opens. But when a new opportunity presents itself, you need to take hold of it, because you are the one who is truly responsible for your happiness. You can wish and dream, but nothing will happen unless you act on those dreams.

- The path from where you stand now to where you want to be can be a long, lonely journey. You will encounter plenty of obstacles and critics along the way. The world will say no to you in a million ways. Hold on to that hope inside you, and it will guide you through the darkness. That little spark will take you where you need to go. If you're not prepared for sacrifices along the way, you cannot expect to achieve everything you hoped for.

- Allow yourself to be afraid. Feel fear. But don't let it slow you down or stop you. Doing something afraid is better than doing nothing at all.

The Power of Thoughts

"Change your thoughts and you change your world."
—Norman Vincent Peale

"Well, I can't help it if I feel this way." How many times have you said this in your lifetime? Now, I want you to ask yourself another question: How often do you reflect upon your thoughts? Like most people, before you go to bed, you probably reflect back on the people you met that day or perhaps the things you did. But how often do you sit back to think about the thoughts you've had in your mind? Chances are, not often. We don't pay much attention to the quality of our thoughts, yet at the same time, we subconsciously allow these thoughts to control us.

As humans, it's been estimated that we go through fifty to seventy thousand thoughts a day. That's a lot of thinking! What's astonishing is that it is believed that up to 80 percent of our thoughts are actually negative. We, as a species, seem to be focused on the negative the majority of the time. How on earth could we expect a positive life with such a negative mind?

Don't be too discouraged; our minds behave this way for a reason. Research tells us that we are more sensitive to negative emotions. Back in prehistoric times, it helped to keep us alive, probably because if we were relaxed and chill all the time, we would have more chances of being mauled to death by a saber-toothed tiger. To put it simply, negative information signals a threat, so our brains evolved to become super sensitive to maximize our chances of survival. Luckily today, for most of us, we're no longer under grave threat of being eaten by carnivorous animals (unless you live in certain remote parts of the world), but that negativity bias still exists in our brain today.

Our threats these days come from a less toothy predator—our own dissatisfaction with our lives. So if you feel disheartened because you've always been a Negative Nancy, take heart because this is simply your body trying to protect itself from threat. The problem with this negativity bias is that it tends to make us take positive information for granted.

For example, when you look in the mirror, is all you see a big red pimple flashing back at you? Your hair may be fabulous, your makeup totally on point, but you focus all your attention on that single pimple. Other people probably haven't even noticed it, but then you decide to bring it to their attention because you're sure that's all they've been looking at. For this reason, most of us are our own worst critics.

"The mind is its own place, and in itself can make a heaven of hell, a hell of heaven." -John Milton

For most of my life, I've let my emotions control me. I mean, they're mine, right? Who else could I possibly trust more than myself? But that's the problem. As real as your emotions feel, your feelings aren't necessarily reality.

The truth is, emotions are like a haze. In the moment, that haze blinds your vision so you cannot see clearly. Yesterday I was on the phone, chatting with my older sister, Claire. We grew up fighting like cats and dogs, but it wasn't until she left our family home to study in England that we grew much closer. It's so cool now that both of us have families of our own, and we have both moved back to Northern Ireland. So we get to see each other much more often, and luckily, we don't fight anymore!

Not too long ago, Claire decided to take a year off work to concentrate on taking care of her two toddlers. One evening, after a stressful day trying to break up far too many fights, she went online and, out of frustration, started applying for a variety of jobs in her field, website design. She had always been confident in her work because she knew she was good at it. She was excited by the thought of having grown-up conversations, waking up in the morning to put on nice clothes and makeup, and heading off to an office. She'd had enough of being in the same outfit for most of the year (her pajamas). She felt ready to take on the world again.

Then a company responded to her job application and requested an interview straightaway. She suddenly felt different. She wasn't afraid of the work, since she was confident with her skills and her ability to do the job; she just didn't feel as up for it as the day she applied. She realized that she had acted out of frustration and made a rash decision, applying for new jobs after a particularly rough day at home. She realized that even if she got the job, minus all the daycare fees, they would only be earning a little bit more each month as a family. She wouldn't be left with much time with her kids either. There would be lots of hurrying in the morning to get them ready for daycare and even more hurrying afterward to get them fed, bathed, and ready for bed. This, of course, is the reality for many families, but she wasn't sure if this was the life she wanted for hers. She told me she didn't understand herself. Why did she suddenly feel so different from last week? I told her that feelings are fickle, that feelings change, that *we* change.

We don't believe everything we read these days, whether it's an article shared online or something from a book or a magazine. We don't believe everything we hear, whether from a friend or from talk radio, and we certainly don't believe everything we see, thanks to doctored photos and amazing special effects. What makes you think your thoughts are completely reliable?

We all live in this amazing physical world together, but each of us lives in our own special world, alone, inside our heads. It's funny to think about it that way, but it's true. And in those strange internal worlds, sometimes we can have very weird thoughts, which is also entirely normal. Every thought and feeling is happening in our internal worlds, and these thoughts cannot be heard or seen by anyone else. Isn't that bizarre? These thoughts are not necessarily real, but they *are* our reality. Our mental worlds hugely affect the outcome of our lives in our real, physical world. So it makes sense to try to take more control over what goes on up there, doesn't it?

"Watch your thoughts, for they will become actions. Watch your actions, for they'll become habits. Watch your habits, for they will forge your character. Watch your character, for it will make your destiny. What we think, we become."
-Margaret Thatcher

We cannot control what life will throw at us. What we can control, however, is our attitudes. You've heard, of course, the oft-repeated cliché: "When life gives you lemons, make lemonade." I recently heard another version, which insists that you should freeze the lemons instead and throw them at people who annoy you. (I have to say I giggled reading that, but I can't say I recommend it! Keep that vitamin C for yourself, baby.)

The intentions of the original phrase are obvious though. Sometimes in life, crappy things will happen. You will be hurt, betrayed, challenged, confused, frustrated, depressed, scared, disappointed, and a million other things in between. But if you can figure out how to add a little sugar to all that lemony bitterness, life becomes a little sweeter.

Because it's true. Life can get tremendously tough, but a negative attitude will only make things worse. Being bitter and resentful won't make anything better. If anything, it will only cause more problems. If you have the right attitude (the sugar) and if you focus on acceptance, learning a lesson from whatever problem you are having, and figuring out how to find the solution, you will recover and move on faster. I'm not saying you should kid yourself and deny your feelings. What I mean is, understand that you don't have to be a slave to your emotions. A lot of the time, it's not life that is the problem, *it's our attitude.*

There is an old Native American legend that tells the tale between two wolves, which I'll paraphrase here:

A grandfather is talking with his grandson. The old man tells the child that there are two wolves inside of us that are always at war with each other. One of them is a good wolf, which represents positive traits, like kindness, bravery, and love. The other is a bad wolf, which represents negative traits, like greed, hatred, and fear. The grandson stops and, for a second, thinks about what his grandfather has said. Then he looks up at his grandfather and says, "Grandfather, which one wins?" The grandfather quietly replies, "The one you feed."

Whatever emotion you feed, grows. The more you feed it, the more real it becomes. If you only focus all your attention on everything that's wrong with your life, you fool yourself into believing that there is nothing good left.

I remember the very first time I joined the gym. It was such an awkward and humiliating experience. I hated everything about it. The weights were all so heavy. The machines were too confusing. I couldn't find my way around and wandered aimlessly among treadmills, weight racks, and medicine balls, completely overwhelmed and embarrassed. I felt like everyone was watching me and judging me. And oh God, the pain! My body ached so much the next day, I could barely get out of bed. I desperately wanted to quit, but I didn't. (I am cheap enough that if I've already paid £25 per month, I will refuse to waste it!) I persevered, and in time, my body grew stronger and faster. Training your emotions is just like training your muscles. The more you work at it, the stronger you get. You can train your mind to be more positive.

Be Mindful: Question Your Thoughts

What does it mean to be mindful? To some people, it means concentrating on something mundane, like brushing your teeth or drinking your tea, and trying to be present in the moment. That's too narrow a definition for me though.

To me, being mindful means a few different things. First of all, being mindful means you, in your own mind, must believe in yourself. When you believe in your abilities as a person, you can accomplish all sorts of incredible things. However, there are also moments we must learn to be mindful by questioning our thoughts. I don't mean that you should doubt yourself, but that you should question your negative thoughts. Studies have revealed that 85 percent of what we worry about doesn't even happen. I still find this difficult to believe. Does this mean that most of the time, we make ourselves miserable for nothing?

But sometimes, your worst nightmare does come true. One of my subscribers, Carmen, became suspicious when her long-term boyfriend started to leave the room to use his phone. Then he suddenly added a password lock to his mobile device, which made her even more suspicious. She knew it was wrong to invade his privacy, but her gut instinct was screaming that something was going on. It took days of trying, but on one lucky (or misfortunate) night, she finally guessed his pin and got access into his phone. When she discovered the truth through his text messages, that he'd been cheating on her for almost a year, she was absolutely devastated.

Her discovery of this terrible news was compounded by the unfortunate fact that she uncovered the truth the day before a big job interview. Carmen had been dreaming of becoming a flight attendant for years, and she had finally made it onto the short list of potential hires for a local airline. On the day of the interview, she was emotionally distraught and fatigued, so perhaps it's not surprising that she performed poorly and did not get the job. The following week, she got into a car accident, and her car was totaled.

With all this bad news hitting her at once, she was devastated and spent the whole month feeling sorry for herself. She had always been a confident girl, but her boyfriend's infidelity made her insecure.

Was something wrong with her? Was she not pretty enough? Was she not interesting enough? Her sadness eventually turned into fear and anger. She felt alone, ugly, and useless; life couldn't possibly get any worse, she concluded.

Around this time, Carmen and I started exchanging emails about all the devastating things going on in her life, and our communication continued for several weeks. I told her that of course it's very normal to experience sad and angry emotions in a tough situation, but that she couldn't allow herself to stay there too long.

Everything I said to Carmen was nothing she hadn't heard from her friends and family, but I hoped that hearing it from me, someone who wasn't part of her daily life, would be just the encouragement she needed to start questioning her thoughts. Once pressed, she realized that her mind had been filled with mostly negative thoughts for weeks. But was there any truth to them? She may have felt ugly, but was she really? Once she stopped to examine all her negative thoughts, it hit her that the problem was the way she *felt* about herself, rather than the way she looked. Her only ugliness was on the inside, a result of all her bitter thoughts toward the other woman.

A few weeks later, her ex-boyfriend made a confession to her. He told her that he had cheated because he had always felt that she was the better one. While she was charismatic, popular, and performed well in school, he lagged in his studies. While she knew exactly what she wanted to do with her life, he felt aimless and adrift. When Carmen questioned his future plans out of love and concern, it ended up making him frustrated rather than motivated. He started to feel that Carmen was looking down on him.

When a fellow waitress at the café where he worked part-time started to show interest in him, he couldn't resist. His relationship with Carmen had grown too comfortable. He suddenly craved sparks, attention, and lust, and he had a moment of weakness. He wasn't actually that interested in the other girl. But she also didn't know what she wanted to do with her life, so being with her made him feel better about himself. As for the other woman, she'd had no idea he even had a girlfriend in the first place. It was one big mess.

Carmen spent weeks furious with her ex. She was angry that he had wasted so much of her time and that she had allowed herself to care about someone so selfish. In her mind, he was the worst human being on the planet. Then I pushed her again to question her thoughts. Was her ex really the worst person in the world? She realized that cheating didn't make him a terrible person; it just meant that he had made a bad decision, a decision that ultimately ended their relationship. Was her time truly wasted? No. They had shared many wonderful memories together.

It took some time to mend her broken heart, but eventually she learned to forgive him. She forgave him not because she was weak and condoned his behavior, but because she was strong enough to understand that as people, we all make mistakes.

She had felt alone in the past, but as it turned out, she had friends and family at her side, cheering her on at all times. She realized that failing at this relationship didn't make her useless, that failure is part of life, and that it is human to fail.

Yes, her car had gotten totaled, but things could have been worse. She had escaped that accident with a touch of whiplash, but for the most part, she was unharmed. As for her job prospects, she had originally thought she had wasted her only opportunity. But wait—was this true? She realized she could always try again, and the thought motivated her to do better in her next interview.

Carmen started to focus her attention on everything that was right with her life. She eventually stopped pitying herself and took responsibility for her happiness, rather than placing blame on others. And thank goodness she didn't perform well in that first interview, because Carmen is now a flight attendant for an even bigger airline. She is happily single, enjoying life, and starting to date again. She remains thankful for everything her previous relationship taught her. Rather than being a slave to her emotions, Carmen took charge of herself. She made lemonade.

Controlling Your Emotions

I spent my entire childhood living in Northern Ireland, and it wasn't until my mid-twenties that I moved to Hong Kong for my career. When I lived there, I would often visit the International Commerce Centre on the weekends. It's an incredible building; at 108 stories, it was Asia's third highest building at time of construction. However, whenever I stood outside and looked up, it was hard to see just how high it extended into the sky. It's never until the car journey home, when I'm watching from a distance, that I realize just how tall it really is against the neighboring skyscrapers.

Being caught up with our emotions is just like this. You cannot see the full picture if you focus too closely on your emotions. To gain perspective, you need to step back and look from a distance.

By being mindful, it doesn't mean you can banish all negative emotions forever. Of course negativity will be stirred up from time to time. When you are mindful of your emotions, you just make sure the negativity is examined carefully, but that it doesn't linger as long or come up as frequently. Being mindful allows you to see negative thoughts and emotions as just thoughts and emotions, *not the truth*. Negative thoughts are observed and accepted but not necessarily believed. Then they can eventually be pushed away.

Having a good attitude doesn't make all our problems magically disappear, but it does help us better cope with the tough parts of life. We should never deny ourselves our feelings, both good and bad. Sometimes, we all just need a good vent to release the tension.

In my case, I'm a pretty sensitive person, so I cry easily, and I'm no longer afraid to admit it. Growing up, my family made me feel like I wasn't supposed to cry when I was upset, but I never quite understood why. When I was a kid, we watched the movie *The Lion King* over and over again, and every time we watched, during the scene in which Simba loses his father, I had to try to hide my tears away from my siblings. It infuriates me that crying has come to be linked with weakness when, in fact, it's just a release of tension inside you, and it's completely healthy. Necessary, even. I always feel better after a good cry. Now that I'm a mother, I make sure my son knows that crying is a good thing. Whenever my little boy runs to me in tears, I encourage him to cry it out while I cuddle him and kiss his tears away.

Be Wise about Whom You Confide In

When you are going through a difficult time, it's so important to talk to someone you trust. Sometimes it makes all the difference in the world to have the opportunity to get something difficult off your chest or to gain another perspective on your problems. Notice how I said someone, rather than everyone. One of my good friends has a habit of telling everyone his problems. He would often phone me to confide in me about something that was going on in his life, and then he'd make a big deal about telling me how highly confidential the problem was. But then he would go on to call someone else right afterward. One time, as soon as he hung up with me, he went on to call my husband, who happened to be sitting right next to me. After that, he called another mutual friend who was also in the very same room with us at the time.

Why is it important not to broadcast your problems to the whole world? The issue is that this style of coping often leads to more problems. My friend was talking about his problems for the sake of talking. With his habit of constantly complaining to everyone he could think of, he focused only on his negativity and became stuck in a never-ending cycle of negative thinking. He thrived on other people's sympathy, but his habit of involving more and more people in his suffering caused more harm than good. The more he shared, the more his "secret" was passed around, as not everyone was trustworthy. His negativity spiral was compounded by the sadness he felt in the people around him continually disappointing him. You need to be wise about to whom you speak, about who is trustworthy enough to help pull you out of your sadness, instead of sinking you in deeper.

The people who will help you out of a tough situation are not always the people you might expect. For example, my best friend, Annie, is my world. We have known each other for almost fifteen years. We are incredibly alike, and she has been my number one cheerleader from the very beginning, as all best friends should be. However, when I'm bummed out, I often go straight to my older sister, Claire. It's not because I don't trust Annie, and it's not because of pride. It's because I know Annie will always be on my side, because she cares so much.

- "I can't believe he did that."
- "You don't deserve this."
- "Want me to hit him?"
- "I'll grab my hockey stick."
- "Where's his house?"

In the past, I would sometimes actually find myself feeling worse after talking to Annie about my problems because she would unintentionally add more fuel to the fire. It's not her fault; I know it's all out of love. She gets caught up with my feelings, just as I do with hers, and we both end up becoming slaves to our emotions. She brings out the best in me most of the time, but when it comes to dealing with negative emotions, we make each other feel worse. After hanging up, I would feel even more frustrated with myself and my problems.

My sister Claire is different. We may be related, but we couldn't be more different. I cannot sit still for the life of me, while she is much more reserved. Whereas I'm the type to blab nonstop, she is a person of few words. My sister loves me, but she would never sugarcoat anything for me. She'll give it to me straight, with zero bias.

One time a few years ago, I was venting about my husband to my sister. At the time, I was not a happy bunny. Why, I complained to her, am I the only one bringing home the bacon? Why am I the only one taking care of our toddler, while also working more than full-time? How come I end up always doing the cooking too? And why am I the only one ever tidying up our house? I was exhausted, and I told her I was sick and tired of being sick and tired. Claire was completely silent for the first half of the phone call. She let me vent until there was nothing left inside of me to vent. Then, after I stopped talking, she said nothing. She spent several long seconds giving me the silent treatment, at which point I started to panic. She took her time collecting her thoughts, so she could give me a well-thought-out response. Then she said something to me that completely blew my mind.

"Lindy, you're not disappointed with Tim. You're disappointed by your own expectations."

Hmm . . . Was she right? But wait, aren't I allowed to have expectations? Before I could retaliate, she went on.

"Tim was always a clever guy, but he dropped his career to join you in Hong Kong to pursue your clothing and makeup-brush line.

Didn't he make a sacrifice for you? Didn't he help hook you up with the right contacts when looking for the right manufacturer? Didn't he manage all the technical 'boring' parts for you, so you could only do the fun designing part? Doesn't he take care of Isaac too? If it weren't for Tim, you wouldn't be able to have the best of both worlds. You get to be a mother to Isaac while doing what you love in the comfort of your home. You wouldn't have time to write this book if Tim weren't there to help you out with everything you're doing. You cook because you say it relaxes you. Men can't read minds, you know. If you want something done, ask him. You never ask. You only expect. Also, when you want something done, you expect it right away in your perfect timing. You need to learn to be more patient. You are only focusing on what he isn't. You need to focus on what he *is*."

Wait. What just happened? My sister had totally shut me down within one minute. She sugarcoated nothing. I was frustrated because I believed I was doing everything. Truth was, he was helping out quite a bit; it just wasn't up to my expectations and standards. He most likely didn't even know that the bathroom was dirty. By his standards, the house probably looked just fine. So the poor guy was probably in his office, scratching his head once again, trying to work out why I had just pulled another Incredible Hulk on him.

Tim and I each have our own way of parenting, because we are two different people. Just because he does things differently than me doesn't mean it's the wrong way. It just means it's another way. Four plus four makes eight, but so does five plus three.

My wake-up call from Claire wasn't pleasant, but it certainly was eye-opening. She was right. I was so focused on the negatives that

I couldn't even see the positives. I eventually learned to be more understanding and patient with Tim. Once I stopped keeping score (mostly, anyway!), I could just focus on doing what was best for my family. I needed to shift my attitude and get my head straight before I could help anyone else. When I started shutting down my naggy attitude, suddenly I had space in my head and heart to be more positive and encouraging to my husband. That, in turn, gave him the positive reinforcement to think about what he could do better for our family.

My husband knows he took a little bit longer to embrace parenthood (I'll talk about this later in the book), which I think might be true for a lot of first-time fathers, and perhaps mothers too. But now he is a fantastic father to our toddler. Neither of us are perfect parents, but what matters is we both know we are trying our best. I have also decided to embrace Claire's advice when it comes to her point about my husband not being able to read my mind. So I'm no longer afraid to ask for what I want. I'm kind of loving it. Today, when Tim asked me if there was anything I wanted done around the house, I answered promptly: "That's very thoughtful. Sure, can you vacuum and mop the house, please?" And guess what. He happily wandered off to find the mop, without a word of complaint.

These days, believe it or not, Tim and I routinely ask each other if there is anything we can do for each other. We have been together for thirteen years, and it took over a decade for me to realize that men aren't mind readers. My friends, you can't expect your partner to know what infuriated you three weeks ago. Instead of bottling it all up and then exploding on them, do it the easy way. Talk to them.

Your partner does not have special powers, nor do you. Tell them what you want.

When you continue to speak your mind, in kindness instead of in anger, you'll notice that fewer things will linger and fester inside you. Recently, since it was a nice, warm day, my sister invited us for a barbecue at her home. Tim isn't a fan of barbecued food, so he asked if he could stay home. Since I'd been so busy with work and my writing, he had been doing a lot of Isaac duty lately. I wanted him to enjoy some quality alone time, so I readily agreed. "Sure," I answered. "Stay home and enjoy some peace and quiet." Although I truly meant it, he actually mistook it for sarcasm and didn't believe me.

"You sure you're cool?" he asked me incredulously. "Is this a test? Am I going to be paying for this later?"

I reassured him for the thirtieth time that I was cool, and he finally chose to believe me. He is as relieved as I am that I no longer play mind games with him.

It doesn't always work out to speak your mind. Last month, my best friend, Annie, came to visit and wanted to vent some of her frustrations about her fiancé to me. She was stressed out planning their wedding, which was slowly creeping up on her.

"Lindy, he spelled *vows* as vowels!" I struggled to keep a straight face.

"I think that's adorable! I look forward to hearing Ray say those magical words: *A, E, I, O, U*." Annie looked back at me, stone-faced and unamused. (Note to self: It's never cool to make a wedding-related joke to a stressed bride-to-be.)

I switched into serious mode as we kept talking. It was obvious that Annie had been doing most of the wedding planning, and she was getting tired of making all the decisions. But whenever Ray did have input, it wasn't what she wanted to hear. So I pulled a Claire on her.

"Annie, you're not disappointed with Ray. You're disappointed by your own expectations." She was shocked, but she listened. That was a good piece of advice to pass forward. Annie didn't need humor; she needed straight talk, just as I had from Claire. As I said, be wise about who share your problems with. It makes all the difference.

Write to Yourself

If you feel that you don't have anybody to talk to, think about writing to yourself. I keep a journal, and I try to write in it every day, just like a diary. It is my private book, and on these pages, I can be as honest and raw as I like without censoring anything. I write as my own best friend, and I try to be compassionate and kind to myself. There's something about writing that centers me. More often than not, when I go back to read my entries, I am able to look at the situation from a different angle, almost as another person, so I can see things more clearly. Reading over my old journal entries enables me to see my progression as I grow as a person. I realize that it's during my difficult times that I learn the most, so I've learned to be more grateful for them. They also make me appreciate the easy, happy times more.

Go Online

The Internet is a great place for advice and company. What's wonderful is you can be completely anonymous, if you wish. You will most likely find that you are not alone in whatever you're going through. Someone out there understands. You don't even have to just dwell on your problems. Meeting new friends and talking about your interests can help to take your mind off whatever you're going through. Another wonderful thing about being online is that it's full of opportunities to learn new things.

Be Kind to Others

When I was going through one rather dark period of my life, I realized how much it helped to focus my attention on others. I was physically and mentally exhausted as a result of, let's be honest, being obsessed with my own little world. I wanted to distract myself from my pain, but I wasn't sure how. I had discussed the dream of helping those less fortunate with people in the past, but it had always been all talk. This time, I wanted to walk the walk. So I designed a tank top that generated fifty thousand dollars in profit. Not bad, right? More importantly, though, I did not keep a single penny. Half of the profits were donated to one of my favorite foundations, Compassion International, and the other half went to help provide relief for the victims of the Nepal earthquake in 2015. It was an amazing experience, one that really stuck with me. A spark was lit, and I ended up finding a true passion. It was my first step on my path to using my YouTube career to make a difference.

Instead of self-pity and righteousness, I kept myself busy, which made me obsess less about myself. Rather than focusing on what was happening to me, I focused instead on what I could do to make things happen for other people.

I could've gotten stuck in my bitter state, but as soon as I opened my heart, I let more happiness, love, and possibilities in. Being kind to others played a huge role in my recovery from a dark period in my life. Just like a boomerang, when you give out happiness—it comes back to you. My hardship became the root of my triumphs to help me blossom in victory. I didn't let myself remain a victim. I took charge.

Now before you ask the question, no, it doesn't mean you need to donate a large chunk of money in order to snap out of a funk or truly help someone. Kindness is a gift that everybody is capable of. You don't have to donate money. If money is tight on your side, know that you could donate time. Perhaps you could volunteer for an animal shelter. Hold a door open for someone. Help an elderly person cross the road. Be courteous when driving and let someone through. Smile at a stranger. Wish someone a good day. Offer a seat. Give someone a compliment. Listen to a friend. Give someone a hug. Help your mom with the groceries. Spend time with your grandparents.

There isn't a single way to be a perfect human being, but there are a million ways to be a good one.

Controlling Anger before It Controls You

It has been estimated that our brains contain roughly eighty-six billion brain cells. Your brain is possibly the most advanced "computer" in the world, yet for the most part, we are only able to focus on one thought at a time. Sometimes your thoughts may drift off and another one seeps in, but your mind can usually only hold on to one thought. That is why whatever emotion pops up in there, if you feed it, it grows.

But I've learned that you *can* actually choose to replace a certain thought with another. I want you to think about something that upsets you. Perhaps a shared post on Facebook made your heart ache. Now I want you to think of something that made you laugh. I'll give you a good example from my life, because it makes me giggle, and I'll use any excuse to share this story.

On Tim's and my first vacation to Spain, his luggage got lost. It was actually left behind; it didn't even make it onto our airplane. And we can't even blame the airline too much, because we were late to the airport and just barely made the flight ourselves. Once we arrived and were told the bag didn't make it onto the plane, they told us they would have to send the bag on the next available flight, which would take about four days. Since we arrived late in the evening, we were not able to buy anything for him either. He had nothing—no clothes, no toiletries, nothing. I, however, had all the contents of my suitcase intact. Long story short, he had to resort to wearing my frilly underwear (it barely covered anything, by the way). I realize this might be a rather disturbing image for you, but for me, it was utterly hilarious.

I'm sure this makes you giggle, at minimum, or perhaps right now that funny image is all you can think about. Since we only tend to be able to focus on one thing at a time, this just replaced anything else in your head, right? See? We can replace negative thoughts with positive thoughts. And we can do it anytime we want.

A couple of years ago, I encountered a rather unpleasant taxi driver. I was out one night for a girlfriend's bachelorette party. We were all wearing corsets for a Moulin Rouge theme. (Whatever evil clothing designer invented corsets, by the way, must have really hated women . . . or waists.) At the time, we were living in the New Territories in Hong Kong, which is quite a distance from party central Lan Kwai Fong, where I had been hanging out with my girls. The taxi driver was obviously irritated by the distance, and although he wasn't allowed to decline the ride, he wasn't remotely happy about having to drive me well over an hour out of city central and the same distance back again afterward. His fury was palpable.

"What on earth are you wearing?" he asked me combatively, sneering at me. His hypercritical and judgmental tone made it clear that he was not asking out of curiosity.

I knew I didn't need to explain, but we had a long journey ahead of us, so I figured I should make some friendly conversation. When I explained the party's dress code, he audibly snorted with disgust. I took the hint that he didn't want to talk. So I took the opportunity to call my husband to check on him and Isaac, who at the time was only three months old.

After I hung up, he started in on me immediately. "Shouldn't you be at home taking care of your child?" He continued to poke me with little jabs here and there, but I was determined to remain nice. I thought being kind to him might uplift his spirit. Nope. No matter what I tried, this guy was out to do some damage that night.

"You're really short. Also, I assume you haven't lost your baby weight yet." Okay, that's it. Did he just say that? This was too much for me.

It was late at night, and I had no other way of getting home, but I was tempted to demand he stop so I could get out of the car. I am usually a peaceful person but that night, something in me snapped. This guy needed to be taught a lesson. So I took a deep breath and gave him a piece of my mind.

"Excuse me? Who do you think you are? I JUST had a baby three months ago. Do you honestly think that, right now, my biggest concern is my weight? If you don't have anything nice to say, keep your mouth shut and keep driving."

I sat back hard in my seat, keeping my poker face intact but completely furious on the inside. But damn it, I was proud of myself. The driver was silent for the rest of the journey home. I was tempted to throw the taxi fare at him, but I decided to keep my dignity. I paid him and thanked him with a forced smile. (Okay, I may have slammed his car door a little too.) He did not respond and sped off.

I've thought about that incident a hundred times since then. I knew I could have retaliated and hurt him the same way he kept trying to hurt me. I was proud of myself for not lowering myself to his level, but I did spend the rest of the night being aggravated. I had not let my hair down in two years due to pregnancy and childbirth; how dare he ruin my one night out like that? I tossed and turned in bed, thinking about the things I could've said but didn't, then rehearsed them over and over in my head. Why didn't I say this in the car? Why didn't I end it this way?

To tell you the truth, I wasn't actually offended by *what* he said about me. I was more disappointed by the fact that he had been so unkind. Rehearsing what I could have said was absolutely pointless. By that point, he had probably finished his shift already and was snoring away in the comfort of his bed; meanwhile, I was still twisting and turning in mine in anger. But holding a grudge drained my energy and only made me feel worse, and it didn't do a thing to change this man's unkindness. As Joyce Meyer, the Christian speaker and author, says, "It's like trying to fight against darkness. Punching into the dark doesn't do anything. You just got to turn on the light."

Instead of resentment, I chose compassion. I truly believe that hurt people hurt others. If he could be so harsh and unkind to others, how kind could he possibly be to himself? Perhaps he was having a bad day and simply needed to vent; it must not be easy dealing with insane traffic and drunk crowds every night for a living. Maybe he just simply didn't know how not to be that way; perhaps that combativeness was just part of his character. It is tough living life with a negative lens. Instead of allowing myself to linger in bitterness over the unpleasant incident, I decided to see the light in the situation instead and try to focus on the things I was grateful for. I was grateful for the time I got to spend with my girlfriends. I was grateful that the driver took me home safely. Yes, he was unkind to me, but it could've been worse. I could've been him.

Even if I'd had the chance to say all that extra witty and cutting stuff I'd rehearsed in my head, there's no guarantee that it would have penetrated, or that it would have changed him at all. Instead of "Why can't he be more kind?" I focused on "How could I be more kind?" Instead of worrying how he should be living his life, I decided I should only be concerned with how I was living mine. And I had handled that situation without resorting to nastiness, so my conscience was clear. My heart eventually softened, and I was able to drift off to sleep.

It's perfectly normal and healthy to feel anger when you've been mistreated or find yourself in an unpleasant situation. Take a deep breath and don't let it overwhelm you. Realize that the anger will soon pass. If you let it get out of control, it will control you.

People often overreact when emotions take over reality. Once, when Tim went out with his friends for lunch, I overreacted in a big way. I was supposed to join them but due to deadlines, I opted to stay home instead. He offered to bring back lunch, and I happily agreed. His friends decided to order the food to go to bring back home, and in the ordering frenzy, Tim made an honest mistake and forgot to order for me. I was so hangry (hungry + angry = hangry, in case you haven't felt that emotion recently!). It wasn't because I didn't get my roast duck and rice noodle soup. In that moment, it was far bigger than that. I came to the conclusion that he didn't care at all, and that is why he had forgotten about me. My emotions (in this case, my seriously overreacting emotions) told me that my boyfriend was an awful person who didn't love me enough. He should have me on his mind 24/7.

When he returned to the house empty-handed, I cried and made him feel very badly about himself. He ended up never eating his meal—he knocked on my door and left his meal outside untouched. In the end, we ended up sharing it. He still teases me about this incident today, although he never ever forgets to bring me food anymore. (The upside of this overreaction is that I think it scared him enough that he now knows keeping me fed is a very high priority!)

This is just one minor example, but it's a funny one. Other times, I've behaved way worse, and I'm sure I'm not the only one. We've all had moments where we later reflect back and think, "I can't believe I did that." I have made countless mistakes in my life, and even though I don't regret any of them, as they have all been valuable life lessons, I can tell you that many of my biggest mistakes were a result of anger. When you feed anger, it's just like rolling a snowball downhill—it starts off little but then grows so big, it can get out of control quickly.

One afternoon years ago, after a supremely bad day, I got home and vented my anger by kicking my boots off. I was not in the mood to bend down to unzip them with my hands, so I flung my foot as hard as I could and like a charm, the boot flew off. However, it also happened to bounce off the door frame, and then it ricocheted right back, hitting me hard in the shin. It was so painful, so unnecessary, and it could have so easily been avoided. My brother happened to witness the moment, and for him, it was the funniest thing that happened all day. Just like my boot incident, if you don't deal with anger wisely, it will come back and kick you in the shin.

You've all heard the advice: "Don't make important decisions when you are angry." It's so true—as hard as it is, we should also learn to be still when we are mad. Remember when I told you that the evolutionary purpose of negative emotions was to help us survive? Anger creates the urge to attack, escape, and hide. It's that old fight-or-flight response. Of course, this instinct came in super handy back in the days when we were threatened by predators, but now when our daily problems are a lot less life-threatening, it's not nearly as useful.

I know I've said some seriously nasty stuff to Tim in the past out of anger. Looking back, sometimes I'm still in disbelief at the things I've said out loud when I'm furious. Tim understands that I've said hurtful things in the heat of the moment and has forgiven me now, but I still carry those moments with me, because I know I'll never be able to take back the hurt they caused him.

Have you ever noticed how your body feels when you are mad? For me, my chest starts to feel tight. My face gets really hot. My heart pounds so hard that I'm sure the person next to me can hear it. The next time you are angry, take slow, deep breaths. It's proven to lower your heart rate, which calms you down naturally. Take at least ten deep breaths and try to focus on the counting and the breathing, not whatever made you angry in the first place.

Another extremely effective technique is taking a nice, deep breath through your nose. Focus on the clean, fresh energy you are taking in. Each breath in symbolizes the positive energy being absorbed into your body. You are taking in more love, understanding, patience, compassion, kindness, and power into your body.

As you breathe out of your mouth, think about expelling the negative energy out of your body. Get rid of all that resentment, hate, anger, jealousy, fear, and bitterness. Picture all that dark, negative energy leaving your body to make room for all that powerful, positive energy entering your body. You can feel the new life in your body with each and every breath. It's amazing how different I feel immediately after doing this exercise.

Whenever my mind starts to fill with anger, I immediately stop myself in the moment. I tell myself, this is just an emotion I'm experiencing. I'm not denying my emotions; I am simply being aware of them and not giving them more power than they deserve. They are just emotions, and they soon will pass. Experiencing pain is part of life. Have the compassion for yourself to understand that experiencing the anger is important, but so is letting it go.

The Negative Spiral

Whereas positivity widens your vision, negativity narrows it right down. That's why whenever you're having a bad day, it seems like all the bad events happen all at once, right in a row. Negative emotions distract our minds from seeing things clearly, thus preventing us from making wise decisions.

Several years ago, while I was still studying at university, I was trying to finish my dissertation so I could hand it in on time for that afternoon's deadline. I'm a pretty organized, timely person, so I had already completed most of it. I only had the conclusion to brush up, and I thought I had left myself plenty of time. But when I realized I had miscalculated my time, I started to panic. I finished as quickly as I could, then pressed the print button and had my dissertation bound in an instant. The drop-off location was on a different campus, so I had to catch a bus to get there (why, university, why?). As I sat on the bus, I saw that I had made a glaringly obvious grammar mistake in the title of my dissertation. RIGHT IN THE TITLE.

Frustrated, I whipped out my laptop, corrected the title page, then did an in-depth grammar check throughout the entire dissertation. Then I made another bus journey back to the original campus, printed and bound the manuscript all over again, then headed back to the bus. I was going to make it. . . .

On the way to the bus stop, a classmate mentioned to me that the dissertation needed to be stitch-bound. He looked at me wide-eyed, then looked down at the dissertation cradled in my arms. Mine was coil-bound. Oh gosh. I still remember that smug smile he gave me when I looked up at him in a panic. I ran off once more to print yet another copy of the dissertation to take it to get it stitch-bound. Instead of waiting for another bus, I had to ask a friend to drive me or else I never would have made it. I handed in my dissertation at 2:00 on the dot. PHEW!

A research study by leading social psychologist Barbara Fredrickson revealed that negative emotions have a tendency to narrow our vision so we overlook the obvious. We end up being more careless, and this results in us making even more mistakes. As you can guess, this of course leads to more stress and more problems. Positive emotions, on the contrary, widen our attention. When we are experiencing positive emotions, we make better observations and maximize our managing and thinking.

Things would've been completely different with my dissertation-deadline ordeal if I had focused on staying positive. If I had made the effort to check the grammar thoroughly in the first place, I would've saved a lot of time (and money—those bus journeys and multiple book bindings were expensive!). If I had checked my emails and read the requirements beforehand, I would've known that all dissertations had to be stitch-bound. My negative mind made me panic and miss the obvious, thus making me careless.

Staying Peaceful on the Road

I'll never be able to understand why Tim loves to drive so fast. He is a fun-loving guy, but as soon as his hands touch the steering wheel, something happens to him and he becomes a road-rage guy. Whenever he drives, he is always switching lanes and trying to figure out which is the fastest route. He is constantly accelerating and braking hard. Don't even get him started on cyclists and slow drivers. When he complains about being in traffic, I remind him that he is part of the traffic too. When someone cuts him off in his lane, you don't even want to be there. He sometimes even tailgates them afterward out of fury and frustration.

When I'm driving, for whatever reason, I always stay calm. I take my time and cherish the moment. (Tim would HATE to drive behind me, by the way.) When he is with me, talk about a back seat driver. He still tries to make me switch lanes all the time, but I lovingly refuse. It's one of the only times I get to be peaceful and quiet and collect my thoughts. I focus on the road, I take deep breaths, and I never lose my temper.

Tim and I drive the same exact roads and encounter the same drivers and road conditions, yet we have very different journeys. While I stay calm and happy, he is often frustrated. I don't need to add more stress into my life by rushing unnecessarily. No amount of swearing and beeping will get me there faster. I arrive to my destination happy, calm, and collected.

Life is like driving. You can stress about the drivers and road conditions, or you can sit back and enjoy the journey. Our circumstances don't make us unhappy. It's how we react to them that counts.

"Where the mind goes, the man follows." -Joyce Meyer

If you take nothing else from this chapter, just remember how important it is to practice positive thinking. Positive thinking is not the same as positive wishing. You cannot wait for everyone around you to change to make you happy. You cannot wait for life to come around and fix itself. It's never going to happen. If you want negativity out of your life, you need to get it out yourself.

It might sound harsh to say it out loud, but the truth is, you cannot depend on other people for happiness. I love my family with all my heart, and they make me so happy. As humans, we are prone to mistakes. We lie, betray, disappoint, judge, and blame, because none of us are perfect. Placing all your hopes for happiness onto someone else's shoulders sets you up for disappointment because, truth is, despite what you think, you can't control others. It's so much easier to change yourself than to change someone else. Happiness starts within yourself.

Happiness is your responsibility.
A powerful mind makes a powerful person.
A positive mind brings a positive life.

Bubz's Rules

- Emotions are just emotions; thoughts are just thoughts. They are not necessarily reality. Like waves, they come and go.
- Like training a muscle, you can train yourself to be more mindful, to choose which thoughts stay in your head and which ones you would like to get rid of.
- Positive emotions widen your perspective while negative emotions narrow your vision.
- You cannot control what life throws at you, but you *can* control your attitude.

Feeling Beautiful in an Ugly World

D o you remember how carefree it felt to be a child? You never had to worry about cooking your meals—all you had to do was show up at the dinner table. You never had to worry about cleaning up, because somehow, magically, everything seemed to get cleaned up after you trashed the place. You never had insomnia. You never felt the need to download meditation podcasts to calm the stress of adulthood.

My son, Isaac, is two years old now, and oh my goodness, is he cute. With his big round eyes, hamster cheeks, and tubby belly, he could get away with murder with me. It's not just his physical cuteness that amazes me; it's also his ability to have absolutely no shame. Now *that* is what I miss the most about being a child. My son can pick his nose to his heart's desire out in public and not have a care in the world, even if people are watching. Last month, whatever he dug out of his nose, he offered to his grandmother as a gift. Zero shame.

Nor does Isaac concern himself with grace. Why eat in small amounts with a fork when you can grab a big handful of spaghetti with your hands? Who needs napkins when you can just wipe your grubby hands on the freshly washed sweater your mother just changed you into five minutes ago? Who needs to worry about dignity when you can just have a total meltdown in the middle of a grocery store over a box of cereal? (Yes, it's true, terrible twos is a very real thing. I've heard terrible threes might be even worse, but I can't let my head go there. . . .)

As a baby, you are born into the world with a clean slate. As a child, everything looks mostly rosy through your innocent eyes. As far as I can remember, as a small child, there was no such thing as ugly or attractive. A man was a man, and a woman was a woman. A nose was a nose, and a mouth was a mouth, and they came in all different shapes and sizes. I knew a nose served its purpose by helping me breathe, but I don't remember being aware that it was also supposed to be a decorative accessory for the face. It never occurred to me that one nose might be considered more attractive than others. Childhood was just a simpler time when we were all able to be self-secure little brats.

But as you start to get older, it's as if you've woken up to a whole new world, and not the magical Disney version either. It's like when Adam and Eve ate the apple from the Garden of Eden, and suddenly they were exposed to that dangerous emotion known as shame. And it seems to be happening sooner and sooner, as younger children start to succumb to the myth of "attractiveness" and have issues with self-confidence at an earlier age. When the rose-tinted glasses from childhood are snatched away and instead we are given a different pair, they seem to reveal all the flaws in the world.

Growing up Ugly

I can't tell you exactly how old I was when I first felt disgust over my reflection. I would like to say it was around the age of twelve, but in a lot of ways, I think that even from a younger age, I'd always thought that I was never the prettiest girl when it came to my looks. My little sister would often be the one praised, thanks to her long, fluttery eyelashes and big brown eyes.

"Oh my, April is such a beauty like her mummy. Look at her eyes! It looks like she's wearing false eyelashes!," Uncle Benny might say. Then he would turn to look at me in amazement. "Oh wow, she has a big head." (This is not a joke; my Uncle Benny was genuinely fascinated with how round and big my head was.)

My dad would then chuckle and agree that it resembled a soccer ball. Well, symmetry is supposedly a sign of beauty, and a soccer ball is completely round, so at least I had that going for me.

It's true. My head is rather big, especially perched on my very petite frame. But it never bothered me because, to be frank, as a child I just never really cared about my appearance. What did I care about? Food, toys, cartoons, and more food. I mean, I always knew it probably wasn't ideal for me to be as vertically challenged as I was, but as far as I can remember, my childhood was pretty darn awesome.

Fast-forward a few years, and suddenly it was time to go to high school. (Cue scary, ominous music. Dum dum dummmmm . . .) I know that sounds overly dramatic, but honestly, it *was* dramatic. Let's admit it, all teenagers are drama queens—we can blame it on their hormones, or their less-than-fully-connected frontal lobes. Even now, after everything I've gone through, the thought of high school is still daunting to me. Some people say, "Ah, it's nothing compared to the real world," but I've BEEN in the real world, and high school still scares me.

Right around when I was set to begin high school, thanks to those trusty adolescent hormones, my once-clear complexion that I had always taken for granted suddenly became infested with hundreds of pimples. If I ran my fingers across my forehead, all I could feel were big, angry, pus-filled bumps. For this reason, I always had bangs to cover up my forehead, but of course that only made my acne worse. Even just typing those words fills me with a kind of dread. I know many people experienced the same thing as a teenager—the feeling that your skin was at war with you, and you were helpless in the face of its fury.

I thought the cause of my acne was due to poor hygiene, so I became obsessed with washing my face with harsh cleansers, followed by even harsher toners. But all that did was strip the natural oils from my face, causing my skin to "compensate" by producing even more sebum to make up for what had been lost. As a result, all that over-washing made my skin even oilier.

Did I mention that high-school kids can be super mean? I heard a lot of racist comments growing up, as one of the few Asians at my school in Northern Ireland. But beyond the racism, here are some examples of the insults—the memorable ones, anyway—about my looks I received during my high-school years.

Shrimp: I got this one a lot because I'm short. Fair enough.

Midget: The height thing again. Okay, yup, super funny . . . and yet quite offensive.

Pizza Face: This obviously referred to my acne. But I like pizza so that wasn't so bad.

"You can fry chips on your face": Because my skin was so oily, get it? This one was quite funny actually. Maybe you could.

Thunder Thighs: Wait, are my legs that chunky? Holy moly, they're huge.

Dick nose: What? Okay, now this is ridiculous. Does it really resemble THAT? I examined it in the mirror and realized it was semi-true. The bridge of my nose is narrow at the top but flares out wide along the base. OH MY GOSH. I have a penis nose.

Cave Nostrils: What? Now it's my nostrils? Leave them alone. They're perfectly norm— OH MY GOSH! They're right. They're so big that bats could fly out of them.

"Lindy Hearts Rabbit Food": Now this one was written on a table, so I'm not really sure what it meant—perhaps I was eating a salad that day? (HA-HA!) But my best guess is that this one refers to the fact that I had buckteeth.

Only one year earlier, when I was still in middle school, I'd had no idea how much was "wrong" with me. Now, suddenly, I was a walking greaseball with thunder thighs and a nose that apparently resembled a penis. I felt hideous. I avoided mirrors wherever I went, because as long as I didn't see my reflection, I would not need to deal with my grief over it. I went for years avoiding making eye contact when I talked to other people. For some reason, I thought that as long as I didn't look them in the eyes, they wouldn't look at my face.

It was at this incredibly low point in my life that I first discovered makeup. *Wow—this might be the answer to all of my problems.* But for some reason, I thought the end goal of makeup was to make my face a totally different color from the rest of the body—I think a lot of us might have had this problem when we were first learning how to put makeup on, am I right? The more orange, the better. After all, every other girl in my school was doing it. I thought makeup wasn't sup-posed to be natural. How else would people know I was wearing it? Wearing makeup meant I was cool, so let's make it extra-obvious by making it look like I was actually wearing a mask. The more makeup I wore, the "cooler" I would be . . . I thought. So I painted my eyes with bright blue eye shadow and coated my lips with frosty, bright pink gloss. I used bronzer as an allover powder, turning my entire face brown instead of merely orange. (Hey, maybe it'll even become a huge trend one day).

When I glance back at old pictures now, I am fully aware that I looked like a cross between a baboon's bum and a sunburned clown, yet I never felt more stunning. I had pretty much the entire Maybel-line range on my face all at once. I'm surprised that, with all that thick makeup, I could even move my face. At the time, there was no way I would leave the house unless I was wearing a full face of makeup.

Of course, I know more now. Now I know that all that makeup caked on my skin only emphasized my acne. It made me look about a decade older too, but I thought that was the point of makeup. Since I wasn't cleaning my makeup brushes, it only worsened my acne, which in turn caused me to depend on makeup more. Major fail.

It's okay. We all go through awkward phases during our teen years. Right? Apparently not anymore. These days, I see glowing sixteen-year-old girls that look so good that I secretly want to rugby tackle them. I thought you were supposed to be a fashion disaster in your teen years. Nope. These days, they have YouTube tutorials to keep them from going off the rails. We weren't so lucky. Let's not even talk about my clothes and hair back then. I was born in the 1980s. Enough said. Okay, fine, I'll admit one thing: There was a tight spiral perm at one point in my youth. LET'S MOVE ON! No? Okay, fine. A few more details: I only wore tiny pieces of clothing that revealed my tummy. I only wore padded bras (so heavily padded, they bore absolutely no resemblance to the actual breasts underneath my armor.) I didn't own a single pair of shoes whose heels were under five inches tall. I thought I was über cool.

Ironically, I actually met Tim during this unbelievably awkward stage. Suffice it to say, it was *not* love at first sight. He even recalls being slightly scared of me the first time we met. Tim was nothing like the other guys I had ever crushed on. He was different. The boy I dated before him was considered very handsome. Tim, on the other hand, was nerdy, short, and pale, yet something about him intrigued me. As time went on, he came to know the girl underneath the eighteen layers of foundation. He saw my heart, and I saw his. At the sweet age of sixteen, we started to date. That being said, he might have liked me, but he was getting slightly fed up with my makeup getting smeared all over his clothes.

"Lindy, you know you don't need makeup, right? I think you are already beautiful," he said, smiling at me through his round-framed glasses.

His words were like sweet music to my ears. Nobody had ever told me I looked perfectly fine the way I was, and you know what? I believed him. For the first time in a while, I truly believed him when he said I was beautiful. Mind you, there is nothing wrong with wearing makeup. Clearly, I made a career out of it—I love makeup! The thing is, it wasn't so simple for me. I wasn't just wearing the makeup; it was wearing me. I depended on it so much that it became unhealthy. Tim never judged me for wearing lots of makeup. He only encouraged me that I didn't need to rely on it to feel beautiful. As time went on, I started to wear less and less. Just like that, I freed myself from relying on cosmetics for validation.

I think I went for about two years without wearing much makeup. I also started getting facials at a beauty clinic next to my family's restaurant, which helped me gain lots of helpful knowledge on how to take care of my skin. I switched up my glasses for contact lenses. My mother decided it was time to straighten my wonky teeth with braces. Then, when I reclaimed my obsession with makeup again, it was in a much healthier way. Now I realize less is more. Before,

I had used makeup to mask my face; now, I use it to enhance my features.

This may sound exaggerated, but it's true. After my most awkward phase passed, quite a lot of people actually asked me if I had had some sort of cosmetic surgery. I took it as a compliment, because it must've meant I looked much better now than I had before. I knew I was not exactly supermodel material, but hey, I was finally feeling good about myself again. While I was a bit of a nobody in high school, by the time I got to university, I became quite the social butterfly, meeting new friends left, right, and center. The irony is that until then, I hadn't had enough confidence in my looks to allow my personality to shine through. Once my crippling insecurity about my appearance got mostly out of my way, I was finally comfortable being myself.

I believe we are all beautiful in our unique ways and we deserve to feel beautiful. For some of you, you just don't know it yet. Nothing is more beautiful than a woman who truly believes she is. As I sit here typing this to you, with my non-matching pajamas, a messy top knot, and a bare face, I can honestly tell you that I have never felt more beautiful.

It's not that any of us are ugly. Society is ugly. We live in a materialistic and superficial culture that's constantly feeding us overwhelming messages of an arbitrary and unreachable standard of beauty. No wonder so many people get lost.

As a seasoned beauty vlogger on YouTube, beauty, hair, and makeup would most certainly be my forte. I have built my entire career out of sharing beauty tips and tricks to people all around the world. So don't get me wrong—I absolutely adore experimenting with makeup. I know how empowered a woman can feel from just wearing a bolder lipstick. We know we feel different when we're dolled up in the evening versus when we're scruffy in the morning. Our posture and even the way we talk and act changes. It's obvious that external beauty can bring self-confidence.

But let's also be honest here. I'm not saying that having good looks doesn't have its perks, because of course it does! It's actually proven that people who are blessed in the looks department tend to get treated better and have easier lives. However, if this is the case, why do so many beautiful, successful models feel so badly about themselves? Are we so focused on their appearance that we don't even realize the hurt that goes on behind the good looks?

Being beautiful isn't the answer to long-term happiness and having a beautiful life. Even women like Jessica Alba admit that they don't want to be seen as just pretty faces. There is so much more to us than our surface. Good looks may open up more doors when it comes to relationships and opportunities, but it certainly does not guarantee anyone a happily ever after. You want to know what lasts forever? A good personality. Physical beauty isn't meant to last; it will fade and fray around the edges through time. But a beautiful mind will stay young forever.

I have spent the past decade teaching people around the world how to take care of their exterior, and the truth is, I know I have so much more to give. This makes me so happy, because today I am now able to share how to take care of your heart. It's time for a beauty rehab. Are you ready to start a new journey to feeling good about yourself again?

We will explore together what it means to be truly beautiful inside and out. Connect to your power and glow from within. It's time you reclaim your beauty for yourself.

Beauty Is in the Eye of the Beholder

I often hear people say "beauty is in the eye of the beholder," but to be honest, I never truly understood the meaning of it until . . . last week.

Tim and I were looking for a wall print for our living room. I was totally digging this framed geometric print because the colors would have suited the rest of our furniture nicely. My husband, on the other hand, was not feeling it; he didn't understand the concept. He preferred to hang something on the wall that meant something to him. He suggested a giant print of the LEGO man. (Ughhhh.) As a result, he and I had completely different opinions of what would look good on our wall. Very much like art, beauty is subjective. What one considers "beautiful" may not be so to someone else.

Some have said we believe ourselves to be 20 percent less attractive than how others perceive us. Get out of here! Do you know the reason behind this? Let me enlighten you. When we look at our reflections, all we see is our surface. What it does not reveal is everything that's underneath. (When I say "underneath," I don't just mean your skin because we all know mirrors show us that too. I always joke that magnifying mirrors were invented to lower a woman's self-esteem. Want to feel really badly about yourself? Buy a magnifying mirror. I hate those things.)

Anyway, back to my point again. Our reflection from a mirror only shows our packaging; it does not show us the personality tucked beneath all that packaging. No mirror actually shows you a true reflection of who you *are*.

On the other hand, your friends and family are able to see beyond your physical appearance. Underneath your skin and clothes, they see your kindness, your sense of humor, your passion, dreams, intelligence, gifts, and so much more.

They see all this when they look at you. And so should you. In this superficial culture, one that so heavily promotes an unrealistic standard of beauty, it is easy to feel pressured. Which is ironic because beauty is meant to empower you, not make you feel weak.

I am a big people watcher. Perhaps it sounds a bit creepy, but when I'm in a restaurant or on a bus, I love to watch everyone around me go about their daily lives. I prefer not to depend on my phone too much for entertainment, so I try to keep myself amused by focusing on my surroundings. When I stare at strangers in the street, it is easy to look at them as two-dimensional puppets. But then you realize that these are real people who have dreams, fears, and aspirations, just like you. Individually, they each have a story to tell.

I am usually in my car when I'm in the UK, but whenever I visit Hong Kong, the public transportation there is so convenient that I enjoy traveling by train and bus. A few months ago, I was on a bus making my way to run some errands when I spotted a young woman getting on board. She was definitely someone most people would consider attractive. She was tall and slender, and her hair was perfectly balayaged and was styled in beautiful loose waves. She was super polished from head to toe: clothes, shoes, bag, makeup, everything. As this young woman sat down on the bus, I noticed a pregnant lady also making her way down the aisle. It seemed like the pretty girl had taken the last available seat, and it happened to be a priority seat meant for the disabled, elderly, and the expectant.

I'd like to give the girl the benefit of the doubt that maybe she didn't know she wasn't supposed to be sitting there. However, I know she was fully aware of the heavily pregnant lady in front of her. As I watched, I saw her purposely look away from the woman to concentrate on her phone call. The pregnant lady looked around, sighed, and made her way to a safety pole. I spotted a few people even pretending to be asleep to avoid giving up their seats.

I wasn't sitting very close to her, but I was so disappointed with the lack of courtesy on the bus, I grabbed my bags and prepared to give up my seat in the back. As I was about to make my way toward the pregnant lady, I noticed someone else had already beaten me to it. It was a lady who was probably in her forties. Her hair was pulled back in a ponytail, and her face did not have on a single drop of makeup. Instead of carrying a stylish handbag, she was holding her daughter with one hand and a bag of groceries in the other. She was a bit overweight, and unlike the young woman glammed up from head to toe, she was dressed in a comfy T-shirt and shorts.

I looked at the young woman on the phone and saw her rolling her eyes, wrapped up in her conversation. She was speaking so loudly that at this point the entire bus knew that her colleague was a suck-up to the boss and that she thought she could do better. I then looked at the overweight mother standing by the safety pole smiling at her child.

Physically, the young woman would be considered more attractive by most people. But it was the mother who was the most beautiful to me. Instead of being selfish, she put other people's needs above hers. She made herself beautiful through the force of her kindness. She may not have been the most glamorous woman on the bus that day, but she glowed from within. Perhaps that young, well-dressed woman was having a bad day, which might explain all the frowning. But all I could think while looking at her was how much her bad attitude affected her attractiveness.

Attractiveness can sometimes be entirely based on attitude. Lady Gaga, for example, is one of the biggest stars out there. Even though some would say she does not have the physical features of the arbitrary mass-market beauty standard, I'm willing to bet that she is easily one of the most interesting figures at every event she attends. She stands out from the pack by being energetic, creative, and bold. Instead of giving in to the typical beauty standard, she possesses her unique style and owns it proudly. On top of her attitude, she is also an incredibly talented singer and songwriter. All these qualities make her fascinating. The shape of her features, or the style of her hair? Who even cares? She is Lady Gaga, and she is so much more than the sum of her physical parts. And so are we all.

Several years ago, when I first introduced Tim to my YouTube viewers as my boyfriend, we received a fair amount of judgment from people who frankly didn't know us.

"He must be rich because he looks like a geek."

"She can do much better."

I was somewhat infuriated, on his behalf, at the pettiness of some of these comments, but they never bothered my husband, not for a single second. You see, my previous boyfriend may have turned heads. Tall, dark, and handsome, he was certainly known to be striking. As good-looking as he was, the more we got to know each other, the more it occurred to me that he carried an ugly aura wherever he went. He was often jealous and was rarely happy for others. He frequently put people down to make himself appear bigger. He only cared about what made *him* happy and tried his best to control me to suit his circumstances.

Over time, he became less and less attractive in my eyes. As you can guess, our relationship fizzled out early. Tim, on the other hand, would be considered cute to most girls, but he is not the conventional "hot" type. But as I got to know him, his charm only grew with the kind words he spoke. He didn't care what people thought of him, and he was always being silly and making me laugh. The type of inner beauty that Tim possesses does not age. Charm trumps appearance.

Beauty is truly in the eye of the beholder. How you are inside will ultimately decide what *you* will view as beautiful. If you learn to see beyond superficial beauty, you will find more beauty in others. And even more importantly, you will find more beauty in yourself.

My Perfect Imperfections

There was a time in my life when I hated the sight of my nose. You remember the dick-nose incident during high school, right? Now I realize that most noses are usually wider at the base because that's where your nostrils are, duh! It doesn't mean it resembles well, you know, no matter what the mean kids in high school say.

I had plenty of other body insecurities growing up too, but it was my nose that bothered me the most. I used to believe my mother that if I pinched my nose daily, it would magically reshape it to be higher. (FYI: It didn't work.) I even bought something known as a "nose huggie" on eBay. Yes, it's true. I know, it was so obviously a gimmick product, but I really wanted to believe that it would work. It was like a mini clamp that would pinch the sides of your nose, and it claimed it could "mold" the nose cartridge for a taller and slimmer nose. I wore that stupid nose huggie for hours at a time when I was a young teen, and, man, did it hurt. (I could've just used a clothing peg for the same results, both the pain and the lack of effect!) Anyway, as you can guess, it was a waste of money; all it left me with was a bright red nose.

I'm ashamed to say that I spent hours looking in the mirror, studying the feature that was "holding me back." (Holding me back from *what?*) The nose is bang in the center of the face, so it's always going to be the focal point, right? I would cover my nose with my hand and decide I looked so much better when it was covered up. For years, I had been so self-conscious about my nose that when I smiled, I would even remind myself not to smile too big, otherwise my nose would look even wider. I know, this all sounds crazy to me now, too, but this is what goes on in a teenager's head. For a while, I even photoshopped my nose (badly) in many of my photos.

After hemming and hawing for years, I finally decided to book a consultation for a nose job. I did not tell anyone at the time except Tim. He was against the idea, but he understood that it must have meant a lot to me, so he wanted to support me no matter what.

"I love your nose, Lindy. You're crazy. It's way better than my turnip nose," he would try to reassure me.

"What? I love your cute nose, babe. Don't be silly." I smiled back at him as I pinched his nose.

"So why can't you see that for yourself?" he would respond gently.

Tim inherited his trademark Ng nose from his grandmother. He doesn't have much of a nose bridge, and the tip happens to be a bit bulbous. He is aware his nose is not his best feature, but he doesn't care. To me, I love his nose because it's a part of him. I still think he has the cutest button nose ever. Isn't it crazy how critical we are of ourselves, but so much less of our friends and family? Regardless, Tim realized that nothing he could say would stop me from going to this consultation, so he agreed to come to my appointment with me.

We were living in Hong Kong at the time, so we hopped on a bus and made our way into Central. I met the plastic surgeon, Doctor Ying, and prepared myself for a discussion of what the surgery might entail. Surprisingly, instead of focusing on the nose job I had booked the appointment for, he told me my nose was not my biggest flaw.

Although not perfect, he said, my nose was actually considered above average standard for most Asians, but it was a bit short. He recommended I try out fillers to lengthen my nose tip first. He took several pictures of me at different angles and uploaded them onto his computer. He uploaded my face into some sort of analysis software, and hundreds of ruler lines were laid over my face. Then I realized that the lines were actually measurements being made, from the height and width of my forehead to the distance between my lips and chin.

"Miss Tsang, it appears that not only your nose but your chin is also on the short side. I would recommend fillers and Botox to emphasize the *V* shape of your face. As for the rhinoplasty procedure, I recommend a different technique that is more forgiving for Asians. . . ." Doctor Ying continued to speak but at that point, I had already started to zone out.

I tried to focus enough to just get the necessary details, but I could barely concentrate, and Tim had to repeat everything to me later. In a nutshell, he was telling me that Asian skin doesn't heal very well, which meant that going under the knife could very well leave me with a nasty scar. Instead, he recommended going under my lips to pierce two holes from below my nostrils. Then, almost like piercing a thread underneath my nose, he would tighten the string to pinch my nose inward for a slimmer shape. It would be completely invisible to the naked eye and could be removed whenever I wanted. In a nutshell, this procedure would be less invasive and less risky.

But I didn't hear any of this the first time around. I was too busy staring at my picture on his computer screen. That was when it all hit me, like an alarm ringing in my head to wake me up to reality.

What am I doing *sitting here in this office?* There I was, thinking that a new nose would be the answer to all my problems, but the truth was, a nose job wouldn't guarantee me an insecurity-free life. I'd most likely just continue to pick myself apart to find more insecurities and have more things to complain about. (Like my short chin, according to Doctor Ying!)

I realized that the more caught up I got with surface beauty, the more I was allowing other people to determine my worth. I had been defending myself all this time, telling myself that I was doing this for me, but deep down, I knew it was for the approval of others.

As humans, we are all multidimensional beings. "Fixing" my nose would only change one dimension of myself. Most importantly, can you truly measure beauty with numbers? What were all those ridiculous lines drawn across my face on that computer screen, deciding which features were too short or too long or not symmetrical enough? I refused to give into that system. In that moment, I decided that I am more than lumps, bumps, fine lines, and marks. I am more than a clothing size, more than the number on a scale, and more than my height measurement. It's not how I looked that mattered, but how I felt about myself that was the most important.

I politely thanked Doctor Ying and told him I'd need to contemplate before making a decision, but I knew I would not be returning to that clinic again. That night, as I followed my usual cleansing routine, I stared at my reflection and smiled at the girl looking back at me. I felt compassion and love for that girl. I forced myself to look beyond my surface reflection and focused on the beauty within.

There is so much more to me than my physical appearance. At four feet ten inches, I may not stand very tall, but I can sure stand out as a little lady with a big heart and big dreams. I slowly turned my head from side to side and realized that there is absolutely nothing wrong with my nose. There is nobody I look up to in this world more than my beloved grandmother, and knowing I inherited her nose made me happy because I'd always have a part of her in me. We can't decide our genetic makeup, but there are many aspects of beauty that are completely within my control. Kindness, compassion, honor, positivity, sincerity, empathy, and knowledge—all those traits are forever beautiful.

Why was I taking my "flaws" so seriously? What happens when something truly goes wrong with my body? What if I got sick or badly injured? What am I going to do then? If I needed to change anything, it was my attitude.

Now when I look at the mirror, I see eyes staring back at me that look for the beauty and goodness in others. I see a mouth that speaks in kindness and ears that listen with care. Those are the things I can control, not how many millimeters too short my nose is. I control my beauty and my perceptions of beauty. And that will never change, no matter how much my physical appearance changes over the years.

Please don't get me wrong, and this is very important for you to understand: I am *not* judging or condemning plastic surgery. You do you, my friend. I believe that as long as what you do does not hurt anybody's feelings, you can go ahead and celebrate whatever makes you happy. I have plenty of friends who have had procedures, and in so many ways, I applaud them for their bravery and honesty. For some, it truly changed their lives for the better and helped them enjoy life more. Cosmetic surgery didn't end up being right for me because I realized that the root of my problems lay deeper than my physical appearance. (Plus, I'll just admit it—I was terrified by the idea of being cut into!) But I knew in my heart that cosmetic surgery wouldn't solve my inner issues, so I started fixing myself from the inside instead.

Still, there are some things I would like to caution my readers about, if you are contemplating cosmetic surgery. Please remember that surgery is not a one-hit wonder, but a commitment. It tends to come with an expiration date, because it's not meant to last forever. Very often, you will find that you may need to do the procedure again. It's not my intention to scare you, but do keep in mind that there is always a chance of risk.

Two years ago, when I was going through a rough patch, I decided I really wanted to get a tattoo. A friend (who has a lot of tattoos) gave me a really good piece of advice. She said, "Wait it out a year and if you still want it, go for it." A year passed and guess what? I no longer wanted a calligraphy tattoo on my wrist anymore. This same rule probably applies to cosmetic surgery too. Don't let it be a momentary thing. You don't have to wait a year, but you should definitely take your time and do your research. I recommend talking to a professional and getting all the information you need before you make an informed decision.

People who get cosmetic surgery are often judged for being "artificial," but trust me, I know lots of people who have had many procedures done who are more real than plenty of "natural beauties" out there. Your hair color may be natural, you may not wear a single ounce of makeup, and your body may be untouched by a scalpel, but if you enjoy gossiping behind other people's backs, you are the phony.

What's funny is, we all know that magazine covers are digitally enhanced these days. Come on, we *know* the gorgeous celebrities we follow on social media are gifted with a beauty army to keep them looking gorgeous. Professional lighting, makeup experts, hair stylists, cosmetic surgery, skilled photographers, enhancing software—they need a lot of help to look *that* good!

Airbrushing is no longer just for celebrities, because now we can do it to ourselves. We have filters that can beautify us in a second. There is a famous app called "Beauty Plus" that can make your eyes bigger, nose smaller, face sharper, body slimmer, and legs taller. Okay, I'm going to have to actually admit I own this app myself—I'm guilty here too. When I'm looking especially rough, I do use it to minimize the look of my dark circles. I also love the "sweet filter" because it makes the entire photo look artsy and mellow, but I promise I don't alter anything else . . . anymore.

Even though we are completely aware that perfect beauty is a false illusion created by the beauty industry to make money off us, we still find ourselves fixated by the idea. Therefore, it can be easy to get carried away from time to time. That's all right, we're human.

About two years ago, I had a work trip in South Korea for a major beauty brand. If you don't know already, Seoul is the world's cosmetic surgery capital. In the neighborhood of Gangnam alone, there are over five hundred aesthetic clinics. Because cosmetic procedures are so common there, you'll often see people catching the train with their faces completely bandaged up. It's actually rare to walk down a street without passing advertisements of cosmetic procedures. Some pictures of the before and after results are truly remarkable. One thing that amazed me about Seoul was the number of good-looking people all around me. Why do they all have such amazing skin? Maybe they really know how to take care of their skin; maybe it's the water or their diet. I had no idea.

One afternoon, after grabbing lunch with my fellow creator friends, I decided to wait for the rest of the team while sitting outside on a bench. I had been walking in four-inch heels all day, and I was exhausted. You remember I like to people watch, right? So I happily sat down and started looking around, exploring the beautiful visual displays of the Times Square mall. But little by little, as I watched the shoppers passing by, I became uncomfortably aware of something.

I hope that what I am about to say doesn't come across as offensive, because it is certainly not my intention. It is just that as I sat there, I noticed a fair amount of women who shared alarmingly similar features. Don't get me wrong, they were all absolutely stunning, but my point was, they all had the same big round almond eyes, well-defined noses, and sharp *V*-shape faces. Of course, I am fully aware that there is far more to these women than how they appear on the surface. But it was clear that many had had work done, and they looked good for sure. I'm not implying they were all identical, but it was obvious they were all following the *same* standard of beauty. On top of this, I noticed many women were also wearing their makeup in the same style. Their foundation was pale, they wore rose-gold eyeshadow, and they applied lip tint only to the inner parts of the lips.

As I sat there, surrounded by all these beautiful women, who looked so close to perfection, walking around downtown Seoul, I came to another strange realization. Somehow, at that moment, I could not have felt more comfortable in my skin. It was such a perfect reminder that we're *meant* to come in all different shapes and sizes. I've always known I was far from physically "perfect," whatever that's supposed to mean, and as I've gotten older, I've learned to be more than okay with this. But in that moment, I felt like I was basking in my individuality. Suddenly I didn't so much mind having a rounder face and wider nose. I don't *want* to blend in with everyone else. I was born original, I was born *me*, so why would I want to let myself become a copy of someone else? If society thinks I should have a tiny nose and a tiny face, then that is society's problem, not mine. And anyone who thinks I should look a different way, to look more like everyone else, can kiss my slightly cellulite-y ass.

My beauty lies in my differences, because I am not like anyone else. I am uniquely me, and it felt incredibly gratifying to know that I was imperfectly beautiful in my own perfect way. How are you supposed to love yourself if you're too busy trying to be someone else? You're you, and you'll always be you, and that's pretty amazing actually. Start to enjoy it!

But I'm Not That Special

During one of my stops on the StyleCon Asia tour in Malaysia, I remember meeting one girl in particular. As she ran toward me for a hug, I could feel how tightly she was holding on to me, and I distinctly remember thinking, "What a sweet girl." She had the deepest dimples I had ever seen. Then she started to pour her heart out to me. She was completely hysterical and in tears as she explained that my videos had helped her through many tough times.

Unfortunately due to the length of the queue, we didn't have much time to talk, but before she left, she handed me a little letter, sealed with a sticker of a poodle. It broke my heart seeing her leave in such a sad state when I knew she had so much to say. I promised her that I would read her letter and tucked it deep into my pocket for safekeeping, to make sure I would read it before the end of the night.

When I got back to my hotel that night, I was exhausted. But as I got undressed and happened upon her letter, I sat down and immediately started to read it. Half the letter was her praising and thanking me for being a great role model to young girls, which was lovely to read, of course. But the other half of the letter made me sad. She spent a couple of pages asking me for help on how she could accept herself more. She couldn't help but care about what other people were thinking of her, and she constantly felt exhausted and defeated.

Why is it that we brush off compliments but cling on to the negativity we receive? It can take years to build up self-confidence and mere seconds to destroy it. It broke my heart, because she obviously couldn't see what I saw in her. She was absolutely beautiful to me.

I eventually wrote back to this girl, wanting to bring her some confidence and some peace. I told her that she, along with hundreds of other people, would actually queue for hours to hug a random stranger like me (which I still find baffling, by the way). My point was, I'm certainly not the prettiest, fittest, or most talented person out there. Why the heck would people sacrifice precious time and energy to come see me? I would like to think that people are drawn to me because I make them feel good about themselves.

Emotions are contagious. When you are able to accept and love yourself, people will automatically be fascinated by you because you exude beauty and positivity. I told this girl that I am far from perfect, yet it's possible to be at peace with myself. At the heart of high self-esteem is inner beauty, and the best thing about it is that part is, and will always be, completely in our control. Inner beauty has absolutely nothing to do with how you look, your wealth, your success, or your possessions. It doesn't cost a dime, and yet it is worth more than anything in the world. I reminded her that she is much more loved and special than she could ever imagine.

So how unique are we, really? Well, to put into numbers, you are approximately one in 7,500,000,000 people on this Earth. Against odds of about one in four hundred trillion (you heard that right), you made it to become the person you are. From the beginning of human time, until the end of human time, there will never be anyone who will be just like you. If you are aching to stand out, guess what? Without even trying, you are already one of a kind. What's the point of others accepting you when you can't even accept yourself? When you are able to see the true beauty within yourself, nothing changes, but everything will be different.

Wonderfully Flawed

Last summer, after picking up some new plants from the garden center, I was stuck in traffic with my mother-in-law, when we struck up a conversation about our skin. I told her that before I became a mother, my hands used to be silky smooth. I had always taken pride in my hands because, despite not paying too much attention to them, they remained supple and soft. Now with the constant washing of bottles and cleaning up of messes, they had become rougher, despite using hand cream frequently.

"Be thankful for it, Lindy. There are plenty of women out there who would love to have dry hands from washing baby bottles," she reminded me.

She was absolutely right. Rather than seeing my dry hands as an imperfection, they should be a reminder of how blessed I am to be the mother of my little boy, Isaac. My scaly hands now remind me each day how lucky I am to be able to take care of my family that I love. . . . (And also, that I should wear rubber gloves, but they just slow me down, so I never do.)

I am thirty years old right now. Little baby lines have already started to seep out from the edges of my eyes. I call them joy lines, because they only appear when I smile, and instead of worrying about them, I tell myself that smiling too much is a wonderful problem to have. I have plenty of sunspots on my face despite using sunscreen on a daily basis. I use what I can to minimize the appearance of them, but when I see dark specks scattered across my face, instead of stressing about them, I choose to let them remind me of all the great adventures I've had.

Without even trying, I used to have a flat-toned tummy when I was younger. Even though I did lose my baby weight, my body never quite returned to its former glory. Despite using belly oils religiously, the skin on my tummy was stretched beyond my imagination. Not only was I left with an army of stretch marks, it also left me with a belly that (in my best friend's words) resembled a giant ball sack, because it was so wrinkly and dangly. (Thanks, Annie!)

No amount of exercise will tighten up the loose, saggy skin, unless I get a tummy tuck. Despite all this, my stretch marks and slack skin are a daily reminder that I grew, sheltered, and birthed a beautiful, healthy baby boy into the world. The stretch marks? I earned those tiger stripes, baby. My saggy skin reminds me that I should be proud that I managed to lose all my baby weight. I'm open to trying new products that might improve the appearance of my belly, but if it doesn't work, it won't be end of the world to me. As for my boobs? They certainly grew bigger during pregnancy and even more so when I was nursing my son. As soon as I stopped nursing, they shrank to resemble two sad, deflated balloons. (You other moms out there know what I'm talking about, don't you?)

But instead of getting too caught up in what I've lost, instead I look at my son and think how much I've gained. Isaac was rarely sick as a baby, and I know the breast milk helped his immunity. These days, he is still a very healthy child. Before he became a toddler, he was nicknamed the "Michelin baby" due to his chubby folds. People often stopped me in the streets to ask what formula

I was feeding him, and I would proudly tell them that it was "my brand." I'm so thankful I was able to nurse my son to be big and strong.

Physically, I may not look as good as I did about ten years ago, but I can tell you that I have never felt more beautiful. As I grow older, the more I realize that kindness, charm, confidence, self-acceptance, and compassion are more powerful than physical beauty. I am proof that physical beauty is fleeting, but inner beauty is everlasting.

You've heard that nobody is perfect right? Thank goodness for that, because now we know it won't matter how hard we can try—it's never going to happen. We are never going to be perfect. Nobody will ever be perfect! What a relief. What a breath of fresh air. It has been said that artists see more beauty in the world because they look for it. You want to see beauty in yourself? You're going to need to learn to see it in others.

Our little boy has inherited his father's signature nose. To some people, Isaac and Tim may not have the typical "desirable" nose, but to me, it's absolutely perfect. My height used to be something I was extremely insecure about, yet my husband adores the fact that I am pocket-size. I used to be unable to leave the house without wearing heels. Even though I do still love the look of heels, I'm rarely out of my running shoes these days. Tim hates being seen without his hair gelled, but I tell him I prefer it when it's fluffy and soft.

I used to get frustrated that he would rarely compliment me when I got dolled up for special occasions. He will tell me even though he thinks I look great with the glamorous makeup, hair, and clothes, he still likes how I look the most when I'm barefaced with sweats on.

What you find unattractive about yourself could very well be something you are loved for.

"It matters more what's in a woman's face than what's on it."
-Claudette Colbert

Less Beast, More Beauty

Having confidence gives you permission to be different. We know perfection does not exist, as it is a false illusion created by the beauty media, using photoshop, clever makeup, special lighting, lots of duct tape, cosmetic surgery, and plenty more. Even the celebrities who make it onto those 100 Most Sexy lists will have insecurities here and there. Even Beyoncé gets pimples. Nobody is perfect. The problem isn't always with the generated images we see online and in magazines; it's the false illusions we generate in our heads on how *we* look.

As I write these pages, I am waiting with huge excitement for the remake of *Beauty and the Beast* to hit theaters. Like many of you out there, I can't wait. Even my husband is excited for it. (He is a huge Emma Watson fan.) Out of all the Disney animations, *Beauty and the Beast* has always been my favorite. If you haven't seen it before (remedy this immediately!), let me explain the gist of the story for you: A beautiful woman named Belle is held captive by an angry beast in a large castle. Even though at first she is taken aback by his intimidating exterior and forceful attitude, she eventually falls in love with him after realizing that deep down, he has a beautiful heart. In the end, her one true act of love transforms him back into a human being, and they live happily ever after. Sweet, isn't it?

Let me remind you that this is a fairy tale; unfortunately this last part does not exist in real life. Instead of waiting for someone to come along and "fix" us, it's our responsibility to discover our inner beauty—no magic kiss or beautiful person will be able to uncover inner beauty for us. When you are at peace with yourself, it automatically will make you even more beautiful. Then, just like magic, you transform. Feeling beautiful has nothing to do with the way you look. You already have everything you'll ever need to feel beautiful. It has nothing to do with your size, or whether you look like a Victoria's Secret model. True beauty is the result of carrying yourself with confidence and power.

Bubz's Rules

- The more caught up we get with superficial beauty, the more we allow other people to determine our worth. You more than a clothing size, more than the number on a scale. It's not how you look that matters, but how you feel about yourself that counts. Nothing is more beautiful than a woman who truly believes she is.
- When we look at our reflections, all we see is the surface. No mirror actually shows you a true reflection of who you *are*. If you learn to see beyond superficial beauty, you will find more

beauty in others. And even more importantly, you will find more beauty in yourself.

- We can't decide our genetic makeup, but there are many aspects of beauty that are completely within your control. Kindness, compassion, honor, positivity, sincerity, empathy, knowledge— all those traits are forever beautiful. Physical beauty is fleeting, but inner beauty is everlasting.

- We are all born original, so why keep trying to become a copy of someone else? Our beauty lies in our differences. How are you supposed to love yourself if you're too busy trying to be some- one else? When you are able to accept and love yourself, people around you will follow suit.

- You are never going to be perfect. Nobody will ever be perfect! You want to see beauty in yourself? Learn to see it in others.

Building a Beautiful Heart

n the last chapter, we explored how to feel beautiful in our skin in an "ugly" world. Now, we're ready to dive deeper into the core of inner beauty for inner happiness. It's time for a heart makeover.

I told you in the last chapter that after a difficult childhood, looks-wise, when I got to university, I finally found the self-confidence I'd always been missing, which allowed me to come out of social hiding and start making new friends. I was being complimented on my looks for the first time in my life, and I thought that would be the answer to all my happiness. If I liked how I looked, maybe now I would finally feel comfortable in my skin.

But I didn't. Something was missing. Why did I still feel so empty inside? Looking better certainly made me feel better about myself. The problem was, pride in your appearance tends to be a temporary form of happiness; it eventually burns out. I had been so busy "fixing" my outside that it didn't occur to me that my inside needed fixing the most. There is nothing wrong with wanting to look good, but when it becomes the only thing you care about, you know it's a problem.

You see, all that bullying I had dealt with in high school had made me resentful. Now that my outside looked okay and my confidence was back, for some reason I felt that it was time for payback and to make sure not to let anyone walk all over me anymore. No more little miss nice girl. Many of my subscribers will find this hard to believe, but I was once mega bitchy, gossipy, and judgmental. I sweated the small stuff and cared way too much what others thought of me. Honestly, I don't think I even liked myself at all then. Despite my increased self-confidence because of my appearance, I still had incredibly low self-esteem.

This little story is to remind you that it really doesn't matter how good you look on the surface when deep inside, you have an ugly heart. What is inside is very much connected to the outside. I believe that it's in all of us to be good. That's why we feel so violated when we see others being mistreated. When you say mean things about others, you know you don't feel right within.

Many times, I convinced myself I was "protecting" myself by retaliating, yet I would often end up becoming my own worst enemy. For the longest time, I couldn't be myself because I was too busy trying to be someone else. Like a snake shedding its old skin, I had to discard my old identity entirely to become my true self. It took years for me to fully accept myself and to start to cultivate a beautiful heart. And as cliché as that sounds, it makes all the difference for a beautiful life.

You cannot truly feel good about yourself if your heart is ugly. We can cover up our blemishes and dark circles with makeup, but an ugly heart cannot be concealed.

Even if you've managed to fool the entire world that you're a complete angel (which I doubt), you cannot lie to yourself. Wherever you go—whether it's to the restroom, the park, the northern reaches of Greenland, or the remote Galapagos Islands, guess what? There you are. *You cannot escape yourself.* We all know how it feels to be around a negative person. Can you imagine being around someone who nitpicks everything and everyone all the darn time? It would be mentally exhausting and no fun at all. Are you that negative person to yourself?

You know the thoughts that go on inside your mind; you know yourself the best. What is the condition of your heart like? Are you content, or do you find yourself getting frustrated easily? Are you happy for others? Do you judge often? Are you always suspicious of other people's intentions? Are you a trusting person? Do you carry a lot of resentment in your heart? These qualities all determine your inner beauty and happiness, which ultimately impacts the quality of your life.

Physically, we know that if we want to keep our bodies fit and healthy, we need to feed ourselves good, nutritious food. If we want clearer skin, we should nourish our body with plenty of water. If we want to develop a beautiful heart, we need to feed it with good thoughts.

A few years ago, I was making a business trip to New York City from the UK to host Fashion Week for my network, StyleHaul. I thought I had plenty of time to spare, but when the plane was boarding, I was horrified to discover that I was lining up for the wrong airline. They had changed my gate without me realizing it—and my actual flight was in its final boarding stages. And, lucky me, the gate was at the opposite end of the airport, a good twenty-minute walk away. My face burned with embarrassment, and I started running past the crowds as fast as I could, like a maniac.

Thank goodness I made the flight in the end. I was the last person to board, and they all applauded me as I nervously made my way down the aisle. Sweaty and hot from that awful airport sprint, I felt so grimy. On top of that, it was a fifteen-hour door-to-door journey from my home to the office in midtown New York City where I was scheduled to meet our network CEO directly from the airport. What I really needed was a refreshing shower to wash away all that dirt and sweat. But there wouldn't be time.

Nobody likes applying makeup on a dirty face, but I had no choice; I had to look presentable upon arrival. So I braided my greasy hair at the beginning of the flight so that by the time I arrived, it would loosen into beautiful beach waves. An hour before we landed, I dug out my trusty makeup bag and polished up my tired, jet-lagged face. I looked as if I was dressed to impress, but I just felt so gross. For this reason, when I arrived, I found myself acting self-consciously around the network members.

After a few hours at the meeting, I was finally able to go to my hotel room and be alone for a bit. The first thing I did was take a long, hot shower, and it felt amazing. It was so invigorating to wash off all that grime. Since I had the evening free, I decided to explore the area, since I needed to buy a few amenities. As I walked out of a convenience store, I bumped into a group of YouTube subscribers. I didn't have a scrap of makeup on my face, and yet I felt much more confident because I was wearing freshly washed clothes, my hair was squeaky clean, and my face felt free without the heaviness of layers of makeup.

It didn't matter that I looked great for the meeting because underneath it, I didn't feel good inside. This is very much like inner beauty. If your heart is contaminated, you can buy all the nicest things on Earth to mask its ugliness, but nothing will change unless you give yourself a heart cleanse.

Water Your Garden

Think of your heart as a garden. If you want it to thrive and bloom, you need to water it with love, kindness, compassion, positivity, and gratitude. If you neglect your garden, all you may get in return are weeds. Certain seasons may come along to make conditions harsh for us, so our garden might shrink at times, but if we persevere, we know our garden will bloom again soon. We can turn life's hardship and experiences into fertilizer that helps us grow and flourish.

With a beautiful heart, we can transform life's ugly situations into beautiful lessons. There's no way around it; a beautiful life can only come with a beautiful heart.

The Power of Kindness

Someone told me a story once that really stuck with me, though I don't know if it's true or just a parable. But either way, it's worth passing on: Once, there was a boy who was deeply miserable with his life. Disappointed with the darkness of the world, he decided life wasn't worth living anymore. On the day he was about to take his life, he was waiting to cross the road when a lady in a car flashed her lights for him to cross. She gave him the most sincere and positive smile, and at that moment, it ignited something within him that told him, "This world can't be all darkness." With something so little, this woman changed his life forever.

At the heart of inner beauty is kindness. When we do something nice for someone else, we receive the benefit of that kindness ourselves. Kindness is a type of happiness that everyone is capable of offering. It's in us to be good, so the more we give, the more we actually receive. Too often, I'll hear people say that being kind is hard, yet I disagree. Being resentful is so much harder. It is exhausting, both physically and mentally, to feel hatred. Kindness is the only thing that frees you from your pain.

For years, I mistook my kindness as a weakness. I thought I was too soft and therefore was constantly being taken advantage of. Eventually I realized it was quite the opposite. It's so much easier to act selfishly and be self-centered, but it certainly isn't good for anyone else, and even more importantly, it doesn't always mean it's better for you either. Kindness is a sign of strength and, guess what? Strong is beautiful.

You've seen diamonds right? They are sparkly, beautiful things that cost an arm and a leg. However, have you ever seen a raw diamond that hasn't yet been cut? It's quite the opposite of beautiful. In fact, it just looks like a big, dull chunk of rock with zero clarity, sparkle, or dimension. It's not until it has been cut and polished that its true beauty is revealed. Although painful in the process, our circumstances shape and mold us to become who we are, so we can sparkle.

You'll often see jewelry displayed over a black piece of luxurious velvet. With the diamond against the dark piece of fabric, its brilliance is emphasized. When you are filled with kindness, like a diamond, darkness can't break you. If anything, it only makes you shine more.

True self-love comes from being selfless. We can become blessed while becoming a blessing for others. You can be happy with yourself because you make others smile. You can love yourself because you are kind to others. The core of this chapter all falls to kindness. Take care of your heart, and it will take care of the rest.

Watch Your Mouth

It's currently winter here in Belfast, so the harsh conditions have left my lips looking and feeling rough. I have even more reason to drink plenty of water and to use a hydrating lip balm, but truth is, my mouth needs protection all year round. A good lip balm can tackle the dryness, but the rest is on me.

Our lips come in all shapes and sizes, and they allow us to do beautiful things. We kiss the people we love the most in the world with our lips. Our mouths allow us to indulge in magnificent food from around the world. They enable us to encourage, inspire, and express our loving thoughts and ideas through the power of our voices.

Think of the most beautiful words in the world:

- Mama
- Dada
- I love you
- Will you be my girlfriend?
- Do you want extra-large fries with your cheeseburger?
- Buy one, get one free

At the same time, we have to be careful because despite our voices' power to build, they can also create lots of damage:

- You're useless.
- You're ugly.
- You'll never amount to anything.
- Go back to where you came from.
- No one cares about you.

It's said that the mouth is like a small flame. It seems harmless, when in fact it has the power to destroy an entire forest. Once the cruel words are out in the world, there's no way of getting them back.

When people say, "We eat our words," they mean it literally. Our words impact others, but they also end up impacting us. When we speak our thoughts out loud, we end up exposing the true nature of our hearts. Just like how you don't plant potatoes and expect to get oranges in return, you cannot expect to live a beautiful life with an ugly attitude.

Guard Your Heart from Gossip

We all know life can be complicated enough as it is; we don't have to make it even more so with our mean mouths. Let's be honest, put your hand up if your mouth has gotten you in trouble in the past. See? That makes just about everyone.

Spend a few days focusing on the conversations you have with your family and friends. Think about the type of topics you find yourself most engaged in. Do you find yourself most stimulated when discussing events, ideas, or other people? This reveals a lot about the nature of your heart.

Let's all admit it: Everyone gossips or has gossiped before. Maybe it wasn't even too long ago that you did it. I'm not here to judge; we are only human, right? Reality shows and gossipy magazines earn millions of dollars a year because they know we demand drama.

Gossip can feel fun in the moment, and it certainly gives you a thrill to pass time when you're bored. However, it doesn't mean that it's good for you. I often get agitated when I hear people gossip. Are their lives really *that* dull that they don't have anything better to do than discuss the lives of other people?

Do I end up doing it myself? Yes. I'm sorry to admit that occasionally, I am guilty of this too—I have certainly stooped low to gossip with my husband or family members. But, we tell ourselves, it's not so bad if we keep it to ourselves, right? Apparently not. Remember what I said? We eat our own words. Even though gossip can be amusing in the moment, it makes me feel terrible afterward.

Back in high school, I used to hang around with a group of girls who were obsessed with gossiping. It was honestly like we had nothing else to talk about. There was one girl in our group who was more outspoken and loud than the rest, and I honestly think they were just a bit envious of her. One day, I was in math class when I heard someone whisper my name.

"Oy . . . Lindy! Don't you think Jamie is an attention seeker?" I could barely hear her question, but it appeared that they were already in discussion about the topic and were now seeking my input too.

With all my heart, I swear to you, I really could not hear what they were saying. I was seated about six rows in front of her and could barely hear a thing, though I certainly heard about it later.

"What?" I mouthed back.

"Don't you agree that Jamie is an attention seeker?" Wow, whatever they were talking about, she really wanted me to agree with the pack. It seemed like this one girl was working hard to drag someone else down that day.

"Huh? Uh . . . Yeah, yeah sure." I still couldn't hear much at this point, so I just nodded and turned my attention back to the blackboard. Big mistake.

Within a day or two, the outcome of that little incident became crystal clear. A few of the girls ended up telling Jamie that *I* was the one going around spreading the word that everyone thought she was an attention seeker. It ended up being a huge mess, and in less than one week, our "group" had separated, and we all went our own ways. Complete friendship splintering, all over one nasty comment and some gossipy miscommunication.

In retrospect, it was pretty ironic because they were all gossiping about one another for the longest time. Then when they found out they were being gossiped about, suddenly they became defensive and decided they were the innocent victims.

Even today, so many years later, I am still confused over what happened. I take responsibility for agreeing with people I didn't agree with, because I couldn't quite hear, I was distracted, and sometimes that's just what teenagers do. But I do feel terrible if I had a role in making Jamie feel badly about herself.

Due to the misunderstanding, Jamie has never really spoken to me since. She even went so far as to purposely vandalize my stuff. I went from being in a group of friends, questionable as they were, to being in no group that day, which in the end, I was more than okay with. They actually all made up again later that month, but I never joined the group again.

Do you ever find yourself getting caught up in conversations where you feel like you are obligated to join in because your peers are doing it? It happens to us all, and I will admit I am far from perfect on this front. But I have mostly learned to shut my mouth before it gets me (and my heart) in trouble. Before I say anything that might be misconstrued, I try to ask myself: Are my words helpful or hurtful? Your words have the power to build and to destroy. In the end, they not only impact others, they impact you too.

Sometimes I hear people telling me, "I just want to feel beautiful in my skin." But then I see them speaking and acting negatively toward others. How on earth are you supposed to feel truly beautiful when you contradict yourself by speaking ugliness to others? It just doesn't make sense. As mothers have been telling children since the beginning of time, if you don't have anything nice to say, then you're better off not saying anything at all.

Saying "She's not even that pretty without makeup," won't make *you* any more beautiful. Saying "Gosh, her butt is big!" won't make *you* any thinner. Saying "He is so stupid" won't make *you* any smarter.

Here's what gossiping proves:

- You cannot be trusted.
- Your life is apparently so dull that instead you focus all your attention on other people's lives.
- People who judge others negatively usually do it to feel superior, which is a major sign of low self-esteem and insecurity.

In a nutshell, gossip basically stamps ugliness all over you. What do you do when you find yourself caught in the middle of a gossip-filled conversation? I encourage you not to participate.

My sister is the master of silence. Her two children immediately turn into angels when she gives them the silent treatment. As you know, she does it to me too. When she goes silent on me, that's when I know I've done something wrong. You see, she is not the type to go with the flow in any conversation. She hates gossip and refuses to be part of it. By choosing to say nothing, she forces me to change the topic. That's another good trick—simply change the subject when the conversation turns ugly. You can be the one who reminds people that there are plenty of other, more interesting things to talk about.

I had these friends who used to go on double dates with Tim and me. They would absolutely go through fire and water to do anything for us as friends, but they also loved to engage in gossip. We have a mutual friend among the four of us, and it occurred to me how much they loved to discuss his life—how he should live, what he was doing wrong, and so on. Despite using all this time to sound "concerned" about his life, not once would they actually do something to help this friend. Truth is, I think they just enjoyed talking about him for the sake of talking. Unfortunately, about a year ago, they had a falling out with Tim due to a breach of trust. It took time for Tim to forgive them, and they have all now agreed to move on from the ugliness, but of course, things have never been the same.

Do your friends bring out the best in you, or do they bring out your worst? We should spend time with people we aspire to be like. I'm not implying they have to be intelligent, rich, or successful. I personally love being around people who are loving, optimistic, and genuine. They exude positivity and therefore glow from within. I find myself wanting to be like them, and they inspire me to improve as a person.

On the contrary, I also see judgmental people who are gossipy and unkind. I don't want to be like them. Of course, you cannot choose your family members, but if you find that your circle of friends encourages you to speak and act unkindly, it might be time to start reflecting. Too often, those who gossip *to* you end up gossiping *about* you just as easily.

When you speak words of kindness, it's like drinking refreshing, clean water. It brings life to you and others around you. When you backstab, gossip, and judge, it's like drinking contaminated water. Unclean water poisons you and your surroundings. Some people are miserable because of the way they are speaking, yet they have no idea. Like a drug, they feed their low self-esteem with negative words as a way to temporarily feel better about themselves. Because it is a temporary form of false happiness, it only hurts them in the process. They can't even see that the negativity they are sending out into the world is affecting them too. The good news is that we have the power to control our mouths so our words work with us rather than against us. If you don't have anything good to say, then learn how easy it is to just keep your mouth shut.

On this front, I have my good days and bad days. I'm definitely not yet where I want to be, but what matters is that I'm no longer where I used to be. What's most important is I'm trying to become a better person, each and every day. Inner beauty, just like life, is not a destination but a journey.

Focus on Things That Matter

Several years ago, when I used to work at my parent's restaurant, I would buy a stack of gossipy magazines every week. It provided mild entertainment and helped to pass the time. But as I grew up, I realized they weren't quite as harmless as I had first assumed. Does it really matter if Celeb A and Celeb B are splitting up? I don't know these people. Does it really matter if Celeb C gained a few pounds? Also, who cares who wore it better? Who are we to judge their outfits? I believe we can rock whatever we want, as long as we wear it in confidence. If they enjoyed wearing it, who are we to decide if they made the right choice or not?

What these magazines care most about is making money off us, so most of their content is often blown out of proportion and based mostly on rumors and even lies. Although it seems "harmless" and you can take what they publish lightly, they often carefully manipulate their words to encourage you to judge.

"But Lindy, they're celebrities. Aren't they supposed to be judged?"

Celebrities are still people with feelings. When we give in to judgment, it's neither healthy nor helpful for us either. I'm not saying you shouldn't read gossip magazines. Sometimes when I'm waiting at a checkout, I'll find myself nosing through the cover headlines too. If I'm in a salon and someone gives me a magazine to read, I'll browse it, no problem. Just read with an open mind and a kinder heart.

Gossip magazines, however, are nothing in comparison to Internet gossip. A quarter of the population of the world is now online.

That's a lot of people! Thanks to the influx of keyboard warriors, information is flying around faster than ever. It has never been so easy to become a target for online bullying. You may think it's harmless to indulge in a little drama, but imagine if things were reversed and you were the victim. Not so funny anymore, eh?

I'm aware that I'm part of the problem, and this troubles me. There is plenty of drama and gossip on YouTube, and as entertaining as it may be for some, it's just not healthy for the heart and soul. Sometimes, certain videos go viral, and I too find myself sucked into certain "scandals" out of curiosity. The negativity ends up affecting me too. I get this horrible uncomfortable feeling in my chest when I witness unnecessary judgment and hate. Whether it's the video itself or the unkind words in the comment section, it doesn't matter—I try to just remove myself from it all. Sometimes, I will even take a long break from social media, because I just don't like being surrounded by drama and negativity.

A few years ago, someone started a discussion forum online that is dedicated solely to trashing beauty vloggers on YouTube. The users would judge the beauty creators' looks, right down to how they think they should be living their lives. Most of the members of this group seem to take pleasure in reading and sharing mean gossip. Some are obsessed to the point that they stalk the creators and purposely leak private information. It doesn't take a genius to realize that the people involved are hateful, small-minded, and envious. These types of forums exist all over the Internet, for every kind of group, interest, and hobby. Even if you are a silent member of a forum like this, and just browsing for fun, I can only caution you to be careful. It can't be healthy to seek pleasure from reading unnecessary hate being spread.

Think how many problems we could prevent if we focused on talking *to* one another rather than *about* one another.

Heineken recently posted a wonderful commercial online in which they grouped two strangers together in a room to get to know each other, before revealing that the two had very different political or ideological stances. They were then asked whether they wanted to leave immediately, or sit down and discuss their differences over beer. It was a touching reminder that it is simple to hate people who are "different" than you, and it is easy to spread hate about a faceless "someone" over there. But when you're faced with a real person in front of you, with hopes, fears, and dreams, albeit different than yours, it's much harder to spread negativity and ill will.

In order to guard your heart, you need to be careful what you focus on. Like a camera lens, if you zoom in, what you focus on only grows bigger. If you focus on positivity, it will develop into beauty. If you focus on negativity, it will develop only into ugliness.

I encourage you to shift your attention off pointless drama and instead focus on things that truly matter to you. It may feel rather odd in the beginning, as if you suddenly have nothing interesting to talk about anymore. Don't worry. Having nothing to talk about is much better than having a cruel conversation. You don't have to talk for the sake of talking, and you certainly don't have to gossip for the sake of gossiping.

There's a saying: "Great minds discuss ideas, average minds discuss events, and small minds discuss people." Instead of being a duck that spends all day long quacking, choose to be an eagle and soar above the rest.

I know we humans are naturally curious creatures, but there is so much more in this world to quench our thirst for entertainment. If you really want to be distracted, take up a new hobby. Join a gym. Watch an actual drama series instead of inventing your own. Take cooking classes. Try something new.

Once you find something that you are passionate about, you'll discover a whole new realm to take up your energy and focus. You'll even find yourself conversing about much healthier and more interesting topics. I have recently taken an interest in baking (*might* be related to my pregnancy cravings), and it has been so much fun sharing tips and ideas with my friends. My favorite type of conversation, however, is when we are able to empower one another through inspiring words of encouragement.

More Encouragement

It is said that people don't always remember the words you say, but they can always remember how you make them feel. Isn't that interesting? One of the best gifts you can offer someone is encouragement. It's completely free yet it means everything.

Here is what encouragement says:

- I care about you.
- I'm listening to you.
- I believe in you.

Many years ago, my first proper day working at my parent's restaurant happened to be Valentine's Day. I was fourteen years old and completely clueless, and I was walking into that restaurant on what would be the busiest day of the year. Looking back, it would've been a lot smarter for my parents to train me on a weekday beforehand, but, it didn't happen. Everybody was too occupied in their own busy world dealing with customer demands to shed insight on how to navigate as a new waitress on my first shift. Fortunately, I somehow managed to adapt pretty well and everything seemed to be going smoothly . . . until about 8:45 p.m.

"Take this Diet Coke to table nine," my mum told me, placing a glass of ice and a bottle of Diet Coke on a very large tray and handing it to me. "Hurry up, the man has been waiting for a while."

"Uh . . . Where is table nine, again?" I asked.

"It's the table with the man and woman," she said over her shoulder as she dashed off into the kitchen. "OY, IS THE HONEY CHILI CHICKEN READY FOR TABLE NINE YET? THEY ARE ON A TIME CRUNCH TO MAKE A MOVIE!!!"

Ma! For crying out loud, it's Valentine's Day! There's a man and woman at *every* table! But my mum had disappeared into the kitchen, so I had to stop one of the other waitresses for guidance. I finally figured out that it was the table next to the fish tank. Ever so slowly, I carefully made my way over with a nervous pit in my stomach. I could hear the ice cubes wobbling on my oversize tray. Even the customers at the table looked slightly concerned as I approached them.

After what felt like the longest walk ever, I finally made it to their table. SUCCESS (or so I thought)! As I leaned over to set the glass of ice down on the table, the entire tray tilted over and the bottle of Diet Coke completely toppled. Of course, it didn't just land innocently on the floor, but instead, it landed right in the middle of the table, soaking everything in its path. Within seconds, it was dribbling off the edges onto the poor man's trousers. This man would be watching an entire movie that night with his Valentine's Day date, wearing completely drenched pants. What a disaster.

"I am so sorry," I managed to blurt out, covering my mouth in disbelief. Thankfully, the man chose to be kind and considerate and didn't seem too bothered by my foolish mistake. At that moment, my mum ran over and saw that I was just standing there like an idiot. She quickly grabbed a handful of napkins from the next table and started to soak up the mess like the veteran boss she was. She even tried to help with the man's soaked trousers, at which point the man's date raised her eyebrows.

"I'm so sorry. This is my daughter. She's new and doesn't know what she's doing."

She gave a big smile to the customer, then turned back to face me. Her expression transformed instantly into an angry, disapproving look.

"You're so useless, Lindy."

She had about a hundred things to do that night, and she'd had to drop everything to clean up my mistake. I know she was just frustrated and overwhelmed in the moment, and she didn't mean to make me feel bad about myself, but her words destroyed me. I tried my best to fight back my tears but before I knew it, I was bawling in a room full of staring customers. (Awkward.)

Scarred from the experience, I relegated myself to the bar and refused to step into the table zone again. Even though I had delivered plenty of drinks successfully that evening, and it was a genuine mistake that could've happened to anyone, I just didn't trust my abilities anymore. Feeling safer inside the bar area, I didn't step outside as a waitress for the entire year. I enjoyed being behind the bar anyway.

Despite the fact that I had chosen this, I did get the sense that I wasn't as important as the serving team. They handled many more responsibilities than I did, and whereas the customers would often acknowledge the servers by their names, they rarely even raised an eye to notice me behind the bar.

One night, two of our regular customers were about to leave. Well into their eighties, they were a married couple still very much in love. We always enjoyed having them in the restaurant, as they were always the sweetest people in the room. As they waved goodbye, the gentleman came over to the bar with the most welcoming smile.

"Without you, nobody here would ever get served their drinks. So thank you, my dear, for your hard work."

It was just a simple little gesture of acknowledgement from a man who barely even knew me, yet it meant the world. Nobody had ever put it in words like that, and I have never forgotten how they made me feel. His simple words built me up.

Positive words strengthen while negative words weaken. Never underestimate the power of encouragement, because it can change someone's life. When someone does something nice for us, it creates a ripple effect that inspires us to do the same for someone else. There-fore, like a chain reaction, that kindness spreads to more people.

Not too long ago, I was waiting in a very long checkout line at a clothing shop. It was a Saturday afternoon, and the store was jam-packed. It occurred to me that it was probably the cashier's first day at work, and she seemed to be having a bit of trouble adjusting to her new responsibilities. I could see the tension in her face as she paced back and forth, waiting for a more experienced colleague to come rescue her from some cash-register mishap. The more she panicked, the more she fumbled. She was barely looking the customers in the eye, but I could see the mixture of confusion, frus-tration, and embarrassment in her expression. The line kept getting longer and longer, and people were grumbling, which only added more to the tension. Finally, after waiting for about ten minutes, she was ready to serve me.

"I'm so sorry for the wait," she said with her head hung low, her eyes focused on the cash register.

"It's okay," I replied lightly. "You're doing a great job, by the way."

At that moment, she stopped and finally looked at me. Her shoul-ders relaxed, and I could see the tension leaving her face.

"Thanks," she said quietly. "You just made my day a lot better."

You know what? Knowing I brightened her day ended up bright-ening my day too. The beautiful thing is, when you make someone else smile, you make yourself smile. Win-win.

Here are some words and phrases we should all use more in our vocabulary:

- Thank you
- Wonderful
- Amazing
- Beautiful
- Fantastic
- You're welcome
- Love
- Hope
- Grateful
- Faith
- Brilliant
- Blessed
- Perfect
- Don't give up
- It's all right
- I understand
- Appreciate
- Forgive
- Kind
- Shine
- Experience
- Motivate
- Inspire
- Empower
- Delight
- Purpose
- Happy
- Joy
- Best
- Strength
- Power
- Well done
- I'm proud of you....

It's human instinct to discourage and find fault. It always feels easier to react negatively when you're frustrated, but the next time you are in a situation where you find yourself about to act harshly, choose instead to be kind with your words.

If a cashier is being rude to you, try to understand that he or she is probably having a bad day. Believe it or not, it's much easier to feel compassion rather than hate. I've been in situations where I've thrown shade in response to a frustrating situation, and it has never once made me feel better. I usually just end up getting even more frustrated myself. Instead, you can kill an ugly situation with kindness. Even a simple smile will make all the difference. Remember, you aren't doing this to get anything back in return. Self-love isn't self-involved; it is about being selfless. Being selfless is deeply rooted in inner beauty and happiness.

Make it a habit to encourage and compliment people around you. When you learn to focus on the beauty in others, it magnifies the beauty within you. When you give off an aura of positivity, people will naturally be drawn to you like a magnet.

Even when we find ourselves in moments of darkness, we can choose to reach out instead. As the writer and speaker Nick Vujicic says: "If you can't resolve your own issues, be the solution for someone else." You will be surprised to know that, just like a boomerang, your positivity will come back to you. Our friends and loved ones are here to help guide us along the way, but let me remind you again: We are the ones truly responsible for our happiness. When you reach out to encourage others, it allows more empathy and compassion to enter your heart. The kinder you are to others, the kinder you will be to yourself.

Be Your Own Best Friend

Too often, we're so critical to ourselves that we become our biggest enemies. As I keep reminding you, why not instead become your own best friend? A good friend reassures you and tells you everything will be all right. A good friend acts out of love to encourage, support, and understand. Remember what I said at the beginning of the chapter? You are with yourself every single moment of the day. You cannot escape from you, so you might as well be your own best buddy. You are the one in charge of your body and mind, so remember to take care of yourself by being kind to yourself.

Attitude of Gratitude

Some of the most beautiful people I've ever met are the ones who focus on gratitude. They don't complain or compare. They believe failure is an opportunity to grow. And they look for the light in every situation. For this reason, I believe grateful people are the most beautiful because they are most joyful.

Too often, we focus on what we don't have, rather than what we do have. We focus on our problems and forget about our blessings. What makes you think you deserve more if you can't even appreciate what you have right now? It can be easy to take life for granted. If you think there is nothing to be grateful for, you are wrong:

- The next time you have a bad day at work, be thankful you have a job. Think of the people who have been out of work for a year.
- The next time you are stuck in traffic, be thankful you have a means of transportation. There are many parts of the world where automobiles are completely unheard of and something as simple as clean water requires walking miles daily under the blazing hot sun.
- The next time you feel lost in life, be thankful you have choices. Think of all the people in the world who don't even have the opportunity to think about what they wanted to do with their lives, because their lives were cut short.
- The next time you go through a breakup, remember that, as they say, having loved and lost is better than never having loved at all. Think of the people in the world who aren't lucky enough to be loved and love others.
- The next time you are a victim of judgment, be thankful. It could be worse: You could be the one judging others.

I am obsessed with counting my blessings, big or small. For this reason, I keep a gratitude journal. It makes the biggest difference in life when you act in gratitude. It doesn't matter how tough my day was; most nights, believe it or not, I go to bed with a smile on my face, knowing I earned yet another day being alive. The sun will rise again and as long as there is a tomorrow, there is an opportunity to love, learn, and laugh.

You see, perspective is important. If you focus on positivity, it develops into strength. An unfortunate situation can defeat or destroy, or you could use it to your advantage to strengthen your character.

Most of our challenges end up being blessings in disguise. The difficult parts of life help us to grow stronger. Even the unkind people we encounter in life can serve to teach us valuable life lessons. From all the times I've been mistreated, instead of being bitter and angry, I've learned that I don't want to be like that. Instead, I am inspired to act with kindness. Even though I've been hurt in the process, it turns out I'm actually grateful for the unkind people in my life. They constantly remind me how lucky I am to feel gratitude for this world.

Less Complaining and More Gratitude

I cannot stand being around people who nitpick all the time. Their negativity ends up rubbing off on me. Complaining comes from an ungrateful attitude of the heart, and honestly, it's a bad habit that's extremely unattractive. How about instead of spending our time complaining, we actually *do* something about it? Complaining doesn't resolve anything.

Train yourself to focus more on blessings. When I was younger, I would say things like, "I'm dreading the long, hectic day ahead." But now, when I try to cultivate a more positive attitude, I'll say "I am going to have a productive day today." It shifts my focus to positivity and makes all the difference for taking on a difficult task.

It's easy to take for granted the people who care about us the most. Think how much better our relationships would be if we focused more on other people's strengths rather than their weaknesses. Years ago, when my husband and I were going through a difficult time, I made things worse by focusing on what he wasn't rather than reminding myself what he was. Blinded by pride, for a time, we just weren't able to see past each other's flaws.

If you really want to hate someone, it's easy—focus on all their shortcomings. Just remember that you have flaws too.

Dealing with Unfair Judgment

Another lesson I've learned the hard way is that it doesn't matter how nice you are as a person—you will still get judged. As Dita Von Teese, the performance artist and model, has said, "You can be the ripest, juiciest peach in the world, and there's still going to be somebody who hates peaches." Whether you like it or not, not everyone is going to like you.

Another question I get asked all the time is, "How do I deal with judgment?" My response usually is, who says you have to deal with it? Now let me use a very silly story to illustrate this.

The other day, my wonderful husband was changing our toddler's diaper. We played rock-paper-scissors, and he "lost." When he finished sorting out Isaac's business, he tried to hand me the dirty diaper.

"What? I don't want it! The bin is over there," I said, pointing to the bin that was equal distance between us. When someone gives you judgment, it's like them offering you a big bag of crap. I don't have to take it. I don't want it. Who says it's my responsibility?

You cannot control what other people say. It's in their minds, their mouths. Sure you could sit them down and go through point by point what an awesome person you really are, yet you still won't be able to control what they think of you. It's what's in their minds that's the problem. Being a good soul doesn't guarantee that others will be good to you. You can't control other people's attitudes. However, you can control your own. You have control over choosing what kind of person you want to be.

"Those who mind don't matter, and those who matter don't mind" -Bernard Baruch

I've had people accuse me of being pretentious and fake when I was just trying to be helpful and friendly. It used to bother me, because I always thought, "What the heck did I ever do to you?" I'd replay what I had said or done, over and over, to try to figure out where I'd gone wrong. Then I finally realized that it wasn't my problem, so why did I make it an issue for myself? You can't please everyone; you just have to accept that not everyone is going to like you in life. What matters is how you feel about yourself. If you base your happiness on how other people view you, you are always going to have a really hard time, my dear.

How are you supposed to live your life if you're always so busy trying to correct what other people are thinking of you? You'd never get anything done. If someone is determined to hate you, they will find their reasons to dislike you, so don't waste your time. Confidence comes from not caring about what everyone thinks of you. You are not a slave to other people's opinions.

Sometimes people will try to expose what's wrong with you because they just can't handle what's right about you. When they cannot control you, they'll end up trying to control what others think of you, which is a sad and pathetic way to live life, if you think about it. They only try to stamp you down because you are above them.

Plenty of people don't even know what they're doing with their lives, yet they often tell me how I should live. I've had people tell me that I'm so cheerful that it aggravates them. People who are negative can't stand being around people who shine with happiness, because it only exposes their darkness and makes them uncomfortable. It's not even that they're jealous of what I have, it's that they're jealous of what *they* don't have: inner joy.

Whether you like it or not, people are going to talk. But no one can make you feel inferior without your consent. Words are only words, and they only become truth if you let them. It's impossible to live up to everybody's expectations. Whether you're at the gym, at school, at work, or on a bus—people will judge. Right now, somebody is probably judging me, and I couldn't care less. You cannot stop people from judging you, but you can stop it from affecting you.

Stop Caring and Be Silly

If people are going to talk anyway, why not just mind your own business? I can go for several months without shaving my legs, and I'll happily wander outside in shorts. Who cares if people might see it and talk? I have a saggy belly that's covered in stretch marks, and yet it doesn't stop me from rocking a bikini. I have and will always have a slightly vulgar sense of humor. Some of the stuff I say might make people cringe or feel embarrassed, but life is too short to be serious all the time. At this point in my life, I am no longer a slave to someone's opinions, and I never will be again, thank you.

Mind Our Own Business

Let's not lie. We all judge, whether we keep it to ourselves or say it out loud. We don't like being judged, and yet we somehow find ourselves doing it to others. I'm not proud of it but like most people, I'm not immune to doing it. I can only remind myself that when I judge someone, it doesn't define who they are, but it certainly does define who I am. We can only try our best to mind our own business.

Let's focus on doing what we can to correct our thoughts. Last week, I was having dim sum with my family. We were sitting near the window and saw a lady jog past the restaurant. Immediately, one relative made a judgmental remark on her weight and how she shouldn't be wearing such tight clothing. Disappointed by my relative's ugly response, I rebuked her and told her that least this lady was doing something healthy for herself. Just like what I did to my relative, we can correct our judgmental thoughts to steer us back in the right direction. In time, it will become a natural habit to look for the positivity in people.

Hurt People Hurt

I don't hate anyone in this world (anymore), but I will tell you guys the truth. There is one person in my life that certainly knows how to grind my gears. Even now, I struggle with all my might not to think negatively about him. He's the type that cannot bear to hear anyone get praised. He will trash talk people behind their backs endlessly and enjoys pointing out everyone's shortcomings. Because bad news tends to travel fast, I know that he has said some very hurtful things about people I care about and me. I'm not even mad; I'm just disappointed.

We do have mutual friends, so occasionally we will bump into each other. But I don't feel comfortable being around him, because I know he can't be trusted. Despite everything, I still can't help but feel sorry for him.

He's successful and wears plenty of designer clothing, but that's it. Under the shiny surface, I know he doesn't have a lot of friends anymore. His satisfaction comes from constantly trying to make people jealous by upstaging them. Think about it for a second. His sense of self comes from making others envy him. That can't be healthy. He may seem confident in the way he dresses and speaks, but despite all that, I know he's not happy inside. A truly joyful person would not speak such unkind words. If his only source of "happiness" comes from making people feel less of themselves, what does that say about the condition of his heart? Self-involved people who put other people down are some of the most miserable people on Earth. You cannot be kind to yourself until you are kind to others. How do you even see beauty within yourself if you can't see it in others? Hurt people hurt others, but they end up hurting themselves most.

When people are cruel, I can only remind myself that there is usually an underlying reason they act that way. People who are hardest to love are often those who need it the most. It can be difficult to be kind to someone who is unkind to us, but compassion makes it possible. Realize that they are damaged and deserve empathy. So remember to be kind to unkind people, as they need it most. This all brings me to the next topic, one that is very important for building a beautiful heart: forgiveness.

Forgiveness

Strength is beauty, and there is nothing stronger than the power of forgiveness. Since forgiveness comes from the family of kindness, it is often also mistaken as weakness.

- *"I did not deserve to be hurt, so she does not deserve my forgiveness!"*
- *"If I forgive, it means I am letting him off too easily. He should learn his lesson."*

I have said these things in the past before, and although it seemed fair at the time, what I didn't realize was that being resentful over past wrongs really only hurt me. There was a person who once hurt me a lot in the past. She did everything in her power to destroy my confidence and happiness. I could not understand why she disliked me so much when, to my knowledge, I had never done anything to her. How could someone be so inconsiderate of my feelings? What motivates someone to possess so much cruelty in their heart?

My disappointment turned into anger, and my anger turned into resentment. All that anger continued to eat away inside of me, completely consuming me. It was unbearable being suffocated by negativity, yet I was the one doing it to myself. With a heart filled with bitterness, I felt ugly inside. How do you feel beautiful with an unforgiving heart? It takes a strong person to say sorry and an even stronger person to forgive. Far from weakness, forgiveness is a true sign of strength.

It is often said that holding on to anger is like drinking poison and expecting the other person to die. We're all born into the world prone to making mistakes because we're not meant to be perfect. What we need to remind ourselves is that when a person does something bad, it doesn't mean they are a bad person altogether. It just means they're human.

Sometimes people make bad choices that consequently hurt others. Some mistakes can be so drastic that they can completely shock a person to their core, and hopefully change them so they never make the same mistakes again. I'm no angel myself, and I've made some pretty huge mistakes in my life that sadly have hurt a lot of people along the way. However, my past mistakes don't define me as a person. Self-forgiveness is just as important as forgiving others. What's most important is that we learn from our mistakes.

Trusting Again

Trust takes time to build and only moments to destroy. But that doesn't mean it can't be built up again. It's completely natural to have your doubts when dealing with someone who has betrayed and hurt you in the past. You can only respect time and let it do its work. I often hear people say, "Well, how do I know he or she won't hurt me again?" You don't. Nobody knows. You will only be able to find out by letting this person back in your life, then allowing them to prove themselves to you through their actions.

You can only have faith, and that's what trust is all about. You won't always forget the past, but the pain will eventually fade in time as new memories fill up your heart. Sometimes, wounds you thought were fully healed can end up being exposed and ripped open again, which can be incredibly painful. We can only remind ourselves that our pain is in the past. Instead, let the "scars" remind you that you were stronger than whatever hurt you. Understand recovery is a process, and it can take a lifetime.

"When you forgive, you in no way change the past—but you sure do change the future." -Bernard Meltzer

Do Yourself a Favor and Forgive

What if you're dealing with someone who is not even sorry? You forgive them anyway, because you're doing it for yourself. It takes way too much mental energy to be resentful, angry, and bitter. Holding onto negativity only hurts you. Even if the other person doesn't deserve it, understand that you deserve the peace. You're not doing it for them; you don't even need to tell them that you've forgiven them. You don't have to see or hang around with them ever again. But you can do *yourself* a favor and forgive. You cannot change what happened, but you can change your future by setting yourself free.

If you're wondering what happened with the girl who hurt me to my very core, I didn't just forgive her but I ended up thanking her. I could have retaliated by doing the exact same thing to her in return, but I refused to stoop to her level. It was not her intention, but she brought out a side of beauty in me that I didn't even know existed. She tried with all her might to break me and yet it only made me stronger.

If I had chosen to retaliate, it would make me no different from her. I don't like destroying; I'd prefer to build people up instead. When I build others up, I build myself up. In this case, I chose to be the bigger person because I wanted to be better, not bitter.

To this day, some of my friends still cannot believe I forgave her in the end. But I honestly felt like I had to thank her because she helped me discover my inner strength. Sometimes I do think about her and wonder how she is doing. With all my heart, I truly hope she is happy and doing well.

Forgiveness is actually a sign of true inner strength. Anger and hatred do not protect you; they only cripple you. If you've been harboring anger over a past offense for a while, perhaps it's time you let go so you can continue to chase your dreams without being weighed down by baggage from the past.

"To forgive is to set a prisoner free and discover that the prisoner was you." -Lewis B. Smedes

Give to Receive

Happiness is like a boomerang; what you throw out always comes back to you. Since kindness is a type of happiness, the more we give, the more we actually receive. The more happiness we feel from within, the more beautiful we become. Therefore, the circle of inner beauty revolves around kindness and happiness.

Earlier in this book, I shared how focusing on helping others ended up helping me to heal personally. By focusing outside of myself, I found beauty from within. The world is a lot bigger than we think, so we shouldn't just focus on ourselves. Make it a habit to reach out to give acts of kindness, whether they are big or small. When I change someone else's life for the better, it also changes me inside. It's a wonderful feeling to know you have contributed to making the world a brighter place. There are so many ways to make a difference in someone's life, and most of them won't cost you a penny.

The Power of Listening

> "Most people do not listen with the intent to understand; they listen with the intent to reply." -Stephen R. Covey

As you might have guessed, I can talk . . . A LOT. I'm a very sensitive and passionate person, and since I love being able to express myself, sometimes I talk so much that I forget to listen.

Have you ever walked into a store and been greeted with, "Hi, how are you?" by a staff member? I'm sure you must have. You probably usually reply, "Fine, thanks," and that's it. If you're extra generous, or in a particularly good mood, perhaps you will ask the same question in return and get the same answer. We often ask how people are without really caring about the answer. What if we made an effort to listen more? I think we would all lead much more peaceful lives if we learned to listen more. After all, as the saying goes, we have two ears and only one mouth for a reason.

Not long ago, I became discouraged when a relative of mine kept speaking over me. She would start a conversation and then, when I would start to respond, she would suddenly completely cut me off and start a new conversation with someone else. At first I thought it was a genuine mistake, but when it happened several times, I started to take it personally. I was quite hurt and wondered if I was even that important to her. As it turned out, she had no idea she was doing it; it was just a bad habit of hers.

Then, when I complained to my best friend about this relative, she gently let me know that I sometimes do something similar to her. Instead of cutting her sentence short to talk to someone else, I cut it short so I could respond faster. I was so upset to think I was doing this to her, but was it true? For about a week, I started to listen to myself talk and realized she was absolutely right. I've never forgotten how it felt to get my feelings hurt, only to be told I've done the same thing to someone else many times.

I've already mentioned my awesome cousin Yannie in this book, and the reason I do so is because I just adore everything about her. Nobody listens like Yannie does. You can talk about anything, and she will commit all her attention to listening and helping you. Now Yannie likes to be detailed when she's talking, which make her stories really good, but sometimes, I'll find myself getting impatient. Sometimes, when I think I've gotten the gist of what she is getting at, I'll either absentmindedly cut her off, or if I'm trying really hard, I'll nod constantly and say, "Uh-huh, uh-huh."

What I hadn't realized was that this actually just makes people feel uneasy and rushed in a conversation. Imagine if you have something important to discuss with your doctor, and he's just busy rushing you so he can move on to the next patient. It would make you feel unimportant, right?

When we listen well, we let people know we care. Believe me, I'm still a work-in-progress, but I am learning to be still. Even though I'm the person that likes to get to the point, Yannie likes to include all the details. Since I love her, I will listen to it all, and it's always worth it.

(I only discovered this right now but the word listen *contains all the same letters as the word* silent. *Mind. Blown.)*

Last month, the father of a friend passed away. I assumed that she must have been overwhelmed by all the condolence messages, so despite offering my support, I thought it was best to give her some space. A mutual friend messaged me a week ago and asked me to step in, since I "always know what to say." Hesitant at first, I agreed to give it a go but warned it might not have much effect. Dealing with a death takes time to accept and recover from. I honestly didn't know what I could even say to possibly make her feel better. Since both my parents are alive, I wouldn't even be able to relate to her pain.

Afraid to stir up more emotions, the conversation started off awkwardly. Turns out I worried for nothing, because me being there to listen was more than enough for her. Even if they were not all the right words, she didn't need advice; she needed company—strong, caring, kind company. Sometimes when we talk to others, we can end up making it about us when it should be about them. Make an effort to listen more and when you do, be present so they know they have your full attention. I have learned that listening can be far more powerful than speaking.

People usually associate communication with speaking, but if a person speaks and nobody is there to listen, is that even communication? Listening is fundamental to our relationships.

When we refuse to listen, we make it all about us. Too many relationships fail today because people are refusing to listen. Instead, they are too busy complaining and pointing out each other's flaws. What if they changed the "You should be doing this to make me happy" attitude to "What can I do to make you happy?" It would change everything for the better, because the focus is on giving rather than demanding.

"When you talk, you are only repeating what you already know. But if you listen, you may learn something new."
—Dalai Lama

To build healthy relationships, we need to make an effort to listen in order to understand each other's needs. One of my friends, Liah, whom I was extremely blessed to meet through YouTube, is one of the most unique girls I've ever met. I had the pleasure of working with her several months ago in Ibiza, and we had so much fun. On the first night we arrived, we celebrated by throwing a huge dinner party. There were plenty of creative and talented influencers there to enjoy a long, loud meal, all eager to share their dreams, goals, and ideas.

Many of the influencers seated around that huge long table were, just like me, extremely passionate about what they do, so a lot of the conversations that night actually ended up being interrupted. It was such an inspiring discussion, and everybody was excited about all the wonderful ideas flowing in the group.

Even though some of the guests stood out due to their bold personalities and others stood out because of their dedication to their work, Liah stood out the most to me. What struck me was not just her beautiful face but how wonderful a listener she was.

I barely heard her talk about herself at all that night. There were even moments when, in the middle of a sentence, she would end up being cut short by someone else interrupting her, but she never seemed to mind. Instead of being overcome by the eagerness to speak, she listened with all her heart. Instead of talking about herself all night, she was much more interested in taking in what others were saying. Throughout the entire trip, she kept showing me her humbleness and her caring heart.

Don't think you have to jump around and shout to be noticed. Liah's stillness makes her absolutely beautiful. Honestly, I don't know a lot of girls like her. In a lot of ways, I aspire to be like her, fully present and calm. Listening to others and making sure they feel heard is a type of beauty and kindness that we are all capable of offering to others.

Become a Miracle for Someone Else

Within the past couple of years, I got to meet two amazing sisters named Ellen and Amy through a wonderful foundation you've probably heard of, the Make-A-Wish Foundation. This meaningful institution dedicates itself to granting wishes for children around the world who are gravely ill. When I received the phone call telling me that this young girl Ellen's ultimate wish was to meet me in person, I couldn't have felt more honored. I couldn't wait to spend an entire day with them.

The girls were flown from Australia to Hong Kong to meet me. I'll never ever forget that day. Ellen, the younger sister, who was eleven years old at the time, never let her illness stop her from living life to the fullest. When they decided to perform a song for me as a gesture, I saw firsthand just how talented these girls were. What amazed me even more was to learn that during Ellen's time in the hospital, she and Amy, who was two years older, often sang for the other children in the ward. They knew that hospitals are depressing places, so they decided to sing and inject some positivity and hope into that space for all the other sick kids there.

Ellen used her talent to make the world a happier place and that made her beautiful. She became better by making other people feel better. Ellen has since completely recovered from leukemia and is now a university student, well on her way to a bright future. She and Amy still perform for children today. And I will always be their biggest fan.

Like Amy and Ellen, there are plenty of things you can do to make the world a brighter place. It makes my day when somebody flashes a smile at me, whether it's a stranger in the street or a child in the park. So smile! You never know whose day you might brighten.

You can always donate to your favorite cause. Any amount, big or small, will always be greatly appreciated. If money is tight, remember that you can always donate time by choosing to volunteer, whether for a church, nursing home, hospital, or animal shelter. My cousin Yannie volunteers to spend time with the elderly in a hospital, and she loves it. She often mentions how much wisdom she gains spending time with all those wonderful grannies.

There are also plenty of ways to raise money for charity if you don't have much of your own to give. But you can be generous every day of your life, not just in terms of charitable giving.

- Be courteous when driving.
- Offer to babysit.
- Offer your seat on the train.
- Give someone a hug.
- Compliment someone.
- Help a mother carry her stroller up the steps.
- Hold the door for someone.
- Be a friend for someone.

The best way to feel good about yourself is to reach out to change someone's day for the better. You might be changing more than one life—yours and someone else's.

Your Story Starts Here

I've shared the attributes of a beautiful heart. The truth is, we already have everything we'll ever need for a beautiful life. We just need to ignite ourselves from within. Now that you're connected to your power, turn on the light and shine your way, beautiful one.

"We do not need magic to transform the world. We carry all the power we need inside ourselves already."—J.K. Rowling

For my thirtieth birthday, even though I specifically asked for no gifts, my cousin Yannie bought me a bath set. It was nothing super fancy or expensive, but it came right from her heart.

"I know you've been working really hard for this book. You deserve to relax a little bit," she told me.

She was right. My back and shoulders had been burning for a while from the strain of hunching over my laptop. A nice, hot bubble bath was, to my surprise, exactly the thing I needed.

It might seem like a simple gift and few words, but it meant so much to me. Very often, I forget I'm a bit of a workaholic. I can't even watch TV without mopping the floor. I thrive when I'm productive, so I end up feeling guilty when I'm "wasting my time." This isn't a very healthy mindset, so it was so helpful to be reminded by Yannie that I deserve to look after myself too. It felt nice to know that your hard work is being acknowledged. It feels even nicer to know someone cares so much about you.

I shouldn't feel guilty about relaxing, and yet I do because I hate the thought of wasting time. Yannie reminded me that time is not wasted if it's going to help me unload my stress. She took a moment out of her life to teach me a lesson I had forgotten, and I was so grateful.

The best way to learn how to have a beautiful heart is to teach it. I want to learn to help myself, just as much as I want to learn how to help others. You have no idea how profoundly you can influence someone with your words, just by being positive. One match can light a thousand candles. When you wake up in the morning, stretch and smile. Spend one day being grateful and positive and sending that warmth out to others. You might find that you'll want to start every day helping others feel better, and therefore helping yourself too.

Bubz's Rules

- It doesn't matter how good you look on the surface when deep inside, you have an ugly heart. You cannot truly feel good about yourself if you don't feel good inside.
- When you do something nice for someone else, you receive the benefit of that kindness yourself. Kindness is a type of happiness, and the more we give, the more we receive.

- When we speak our thoughts out loud, we end up exposing the true nature of our hearts. Your words have the power to build and to destroy. In the end, they not only impact others, they impact you too.
- It is said that people don't always remember the words you say, but they can always remember how you make them feel. Positive words strengthen while negative words weaken. Never underestimate the power of encouragement, because it can change someone's life.
- Focus on gratitude. Look for the light in every situation. If you really want to hate someone, it's easy—just focus on all their shortcomings. When you judge someone, it doesn't define who they are, but it certainly does define who you are.
- Whether you like it or not, people are going to talk. But no one can make you feel inferior without your consent. You can't control other people's attitudes. You can only control what kind of person you want to be.
- Holding on to anger is like drinking poison and expecting the other person to die. It takes way too much mental energy to be resentful, angry, and bitter. Holding on to negativity only hurts you. You cannot change what happened, but you can change your future by setting yourself free.
- The best way to learn how to have a beautiful heart is to teach it. Spend one day being grateful and positive and sending that warmth out to others. You might find that you'll want to start every day helping others feel better, and therefore helping yourself too.

Rising Again

I t would be impossible for me to write this book without sharing a story about the importance of getting up again when life drags you down in the dirt. Everything we have discussed in this book so far—taking control of your life, making room for positive thoughts, not letting fear of failure stop you—wouldn't be worth much if we didn't also talk about how to overcome failure when it happens. You cannot risk it all if you cannot also learn to rise from the ashes.

Sometimes, when you feel like you are running full speed at the world, hitting life goal after life goal, a ditch will suddenly appear out of nowhere. Maybe there were warning signs all along, but you were too busy charging ahead. And you'll fall, you'll fall hard, and it'll hurt.

Don't we all wish we could have a pain-free life? Sure, but the truth is, failure and adversity are part of life. How could we appreciate the good times without the hard times? We cannot appreciate the light without darkness.

In 2014, Tim and I welcomed our infant son into the world. It should've been the most amazing year of my life, but I felt I had suddenly fallen into a cold, hard pit. There were so many precious moments, ones when I marveled at the milestones my amazing son was hitting. But there were also many painful moments, ones in which I seriously doubted if I'd ever be happy again.

What I'm about to share is something I've never opened up to my YouTube subscribers about before. As painful as it is for me to tear open these old wounds again, I know it will be worth it. I hope this story inspires you to keep going when life gets tough. As I started writing this story, I realized that as with all stories, there are two sides to this one. So I asked Tim if he would be willing to write about this topic too. It was just as hard on him as it was on me, and we both feel it's important for our readers to get an unbiased story. So here we go . . .

My husband Tim and I had always been the epitome of the ultimate couple. We met as childhood sweethearts and married after ten amazing years of dating. People who know us both will tell you that we rarely argued. We are both easygoing optimists, and in so many ways, we fit together like a jigsaw puzzle. Of course we had plenty of ups and downs, but we somehow always found a way to come back to each other.

In 2013, only four months after our beautiful wedding, I became pregnant. It was a bit of a surprise! But as shocked as we were, we were also over the moon. Seems like the perfect story, doesn't it? Bear with me.

You hear stories about women becoming depressed about their sudden weight gain when they're pregnant, but I loved watching my belly grow. In fact, the more it grew, the happier I became. I'll always remember how joyful it was, planning the nursery with my husband. We cherished our time together even more and went on as many dates as possible before my delivery. I can honestly tell you that during my pregnancy was when I felt closest to my husband.

My bump grew so enormous that people often thought I was carrying twins. In fact, even my doctors grew concerned toward the end and had to induce my delivery early. But Tim and I were ready. We were so excited for the next chapter of our lives and envisioned our life as a perfect family of three.

Of course, before Isaac's birth, I had read countless books on parenthood, but nothing prepared us for the days to come. Before having a baby, to be honest, I had never realized what a workaholic I was. But just after I had given birth to a little human being, while my body was still recovering from a fresh cesarean, I had every reason to slow down, and yet I couldn't.

When you're a full-time YouTuber, you don't get granted maternity leave. Nobody is going to be able to run your channel if you're not there to film and edit. When you stop, so does your livelihood. I had been uploading consistently for several years, and as crazy as it sounds, the thought of breaking that routine terrified me. It was incredibly foolish, but instead of embracing my new life, I tried with all my might to cling to my old one.

I had always been the breadwinner in our family, so now with a newborn baby in the equation, I was even more anxious about sustaining our future. The voice in my head kept repeating, *"If I don't work, who will?"* I was not prepared to stop.

Looking back, I wish I had spent more time embracing the joys of motherhood, but I was too busy being a nervous wreck. Running on just a couple hours of sleep a day, I became emotionally and physically exhausted. Deep inside, I knew I was dealing with postpartum depression, but I didn't want to admit it out loud to anyone because that would mean I would have to stop and deal with it. As long as I denied it, I would not have to face it.

Ironically, I was the one who panicked throughout the pregnancy. I was anxious about whether I'd ever be a good enough mother to raise a decent human being. Tim, on the other hand, was calm throughout the pregnancy, but when our child was born, it was a whole other story. It was as if all my worrying and panicking had perfectly prepared me for the job of motherhood. My maternal instincts somehow magically kicked into gear the second I held my child in my arms. Tim, however, was hit hard when our child was born. He was totally unprepared.

Let me give you a little backstory on Tim. Before Isaac came along, Tim enjoyed socializing with his friends a lot. Many would describe Tim as loyal, friendly, and generous—someone who would do anything for a friend, which is completely true. He also has always had a LOT of friends.

Throughout university, Tim loved being social with his buddies and always enjoyed a good drink or two . . . or ten. For a petite Asian guy, he could outdrink many of his peers much bigger than he was, which isn't something I was necessarily proud of, but he seemed to be. As you can guess, we've had our fair share of arguments over our decade together over his drinking. I was always put off by how bossy and arrogant he would become under the influence of alcohol. I know this man to his very core, but when there was alcohol in his body, he would become a stranger to me. I did not like intoxicated Tim.

Some people know to slow down on the drinks when they feel tipsy or merry. Tim never knew when to stop. I often worried that he would get himself into trouble, as there were many moments he would get himself into a fight due to his drunken state. When we moved to Hong Kong, which has a reputation as a hard-partying city, the drinking became a frequent thing. Our friends worked long, hard hours in Hong Kong, so when the weekend rolled in, they liked to unwind with a few drinks—usually more than a few drinks.

During those years, there were many nights when Tim would black out in the streets. Some mornings, he would wake up in our apartment completely unaware of how he had even gotten home in the first place. Of course, I didn't want to be a nagging, controlling, bossy wife. And of course, I wanted my husband to have a good time with his friends. But I believed he should put his safety first. As a grown adult, I could only express my concerns (frequently), then trust that he would come to make wise choices. When we discussed the topic, he would always reassure me that there was nothing to worry about. But as soon as we had a baby on the way, I cautioned him that things would have to change, and soon. Even though his drinking had always been an issue in our relationship, we didn't realize how seriously it would impact us after the birth of our son.

Tim:

Throughout Lindy's pregnancy, I was over the moon. We were the happiest I thought we could ever be. Of course, there were times during the pregnancy when we would both be worried—for example, around twelve weeks, when Isaac was falsely flagged for Down syndrome—but all those things just brought Lindy and me closer together. I thought we were stronger than ever. Sure, there are days when a pregnant woman will drive you completely insane with the mood swings or the craving for a certain type of food. But at the end of the day, you just have to remind yourself that your wife is probably growing an eyeball, or that building a baby all day every day is so draining that she NEEDS the remaining half of your cola. . . . So you can't get angry or annoyed.

As Lindy said, I had always had a very active (albeit unhealthy) social life in which I would meet my friends to have a few drinks (yes, I admit, with the intention of getting drunk). Don't ask me why, because even to this day I can't give you an answer. Maybe it was to prove to others I could out-drink them, and in turn this would earn their respect, a sense of acknowledgement. Maybe it was out of habit, as it was something I did regularly throughout university with my peers, mostly to fit in. But whatever the reason, it had become an integral part of my life. This, of course, did not sit well with Lindy over the years. At first the problems were minor, as we were both young and it was somehow the "cool," socially acceptable thing to do. Lindy even enjoyed the occasional drink.

Even though we had argued frequently over my behavior while drinking, Lindy and I always managed to work it out and move on. . . . Or so I thought! I don't want to speak for other fathers out there, so this will just be from my own perspective. Throughout Lindy's pregnancy, although I was extremely happy about the baby, I didn't feel the need or urge to do much else in preparation for a newborn. All the basic things were taken care of: getting the nursery decorated, picking out cribs and strollers, washing the newborn clothes, and most importantly being attentive to your ever-growing wife's needs, whose mood swings are increasing at the same rate the baby grows. But all in all, it was a wonderful time in our lives. And what is important here is the mention of that highly elusive word *time*. . . .

Lindy:

The first week Isaac entered our lives, I noticed Tim and I were suddenly snapping at each other, something we had never done before. For the first time, we were rolling our eyes at each other. But I was concerned and frustrated, not to mention exhausted. Tim was clearly not bonding with our child. He was acting distant and didn't seem to want to be with us. I really wanted to be patient and understanding, but with my raging hormones, I gave in to my negative emotions.

One morning, after spending all night struggling with a frustrated newborn baby who was refusing to sleep, I stumbled deliriously into our bedroom to find my husband still fast asleep. I had barely managed more than a few hours of sleep over the past few days, and here he was, polishing off the last of his nine hours straight in peaceful bliss. I was furious. Why did he have it so easy? Couldn't he see that I was exhausted and struggling? Didn't he know that I also had work and chores? Feeling completely taken advantage of, I went berserk on him.

Tim promised to make some changes. But another morning a week or two later, I was awoken by a large bang, followed by a baby screaming. I opened my eyes in a panic to find my little newborn face-planted on the floor. Tim had been trying to rock Isaac back to sleep but had underestimated his strength. The entire baby podster (which looked sort of like a mini beanbag) had tipped over, and Isaac had landed on the floor. I picked up our son to see an enormous bruise already forming on his forehead. So once again, I completely lost it. For the first time in my life, I swore at my husband for being so careless.

I'm sure there were many moments Tim did well as a father in those early months, but if I'm being honest, I only remember the moments when he fell way short of my expectations. I know Tim was making an effort to be more helpful, but since Isaac was completely dependent on me for feeding, Tim felt, as so many new fathers do, powerless and sort of lost.

This might come as a shock to some of you, but Tim will admit that he did not exactly feel love for his child until several months after his birth. Mind you, Isaac was formed inside me, so you could say he was already a part of me long before he was born. But to Tim, Isaac felt like a stranger. He didn't "glow" holding his son. At the moment, he would have told you that he loved our dogs more, and he would've been serious. Everything he said he would be as a father, he wasn't. I don't know why they haven't come up with a term for male post-partum syndrome, but if there is such a thing, Tim definitely had it in spades.

Instead of understanding and trying to help him through his difficulties, I judged him for it. Instead of being more patient with Tim, I breathed down his neck, which only succeeded in making him feel very unsure around Isaac. As first-time parents, we were bound to make lots of mistakes, as we all do. But instead of being forgiving to my husband, I took it personally and held it against him.

Tim:

I cannot stress this enough: Sleep deprivation, a phrase used often by new parents, is REAL, and it cannot be taken lightly. Lindy and I were so used to having a "work at home" lifestyle, with a schedule where we could sleep for hours on end and wake up whenever we wanted. Suddenly (for me, anyway) this new schedule with a newborn was a huge change; it (obviously) threw our usual routine completely off. Initially, I thought, *Okay, I will embrace this change for the first week or two; this is what it's all about. Soon enough, we will sleep more once the baby settles in.* But guess what? The baby never "settles in." Once you become parents, you realize there will be milestone after milestone. And it feels as if you might never sleep again for the rest of your life.

With all this change, it led to another aspect of my life feeling empty: my social life. For such a big part of my adult years, having close friends was very important to me. Every weekend, I was used to getting a barrage of messages, as we all checked in to ask one another when to meet up, what to eat, where to go, and what to do. It kept my life (back then) in balance.

This is where Lindy and I started drifting the most. There were a lot of things in play—our different attitudes toward our newborn, our expectations of how we each would be as parents, how we made use of our time, how we got things done around the house, our work schedules and priorities—basically every aspect of our lives came into question.

This is the point now where I need to stick my hand up in the air and admit this: I messed up. Because I did. I messed up big-time, because I was just so unprepared. More importantly, I didn't understand, or want to understand, what my wife needed the most at that time: a man. At heart, when Isaac was born, I was still a boy. I'll admit it. I was so immature. I wanted so badly to hold onto my unhealthy social life, but somehow still be a father.

As time passed and Isaac turned seven days, then twenty-one days, then forty days, then sixty days (yes, like all new parents, we were obsessively date-counting to see when he would hit the next milestone, mainly in the hopes that he would soon sleep longer), my patience grew thinner. My attitude was negative, and my words were harsh. I was feeling resentful toward my two-month-old son, who was still not giving either of us much sleep, and Lindy substantially less due to Isaac being exclusively breastfed.

Lindy:

For the first six months of Isaac's life, I felt like I did everything on my own. The more disappointed I became, the more resentful I grew. To me, I felt like I'd had all the responsibilities dumped on me. And I started keeping score, one of the most dangerous things one can do in a marriage.

While Tim was continuing to go out drinking until the early hours of the morning, my heart only grew harder. I never thought it would ever come to this, but suddenly I was every bit the nagging wife. I begged him to "grow up" for the sake of our family. The more I tried to change him, the more reluctant he became.

Even though we were living under the same roof, we could not have been leading more separate lives. I realized the more I cared, the more anger I would feel. So I chose to give up on him. I thought, *The less I expect, the less I'll be disappointed.* Instead, I buried myself in taking care of Isaac, while filling up any spare time I could manage with work projects to distract myself from our issues. I'm sure it won't be a surprise to learn that this was *not* a solution. I was sticking a Band-Aid over a bullet hole. It didn't work.

I was so busy taking care of our son and maintaining our livelihood that I forgot how to be a wife to my husband. My husband grew bitter that this little human had come along and suddenly taken away his life AND his wife. He had always known how to take care of me, but now he couldn't even recognize his wife, who had suddenly become so resentful.

Tim:

You know all those wonderful stories of fathers who "fall in love" with their child immediately as soon as they hold their baby for the first time? I am going to be totally honest. I am guilty of NOT being one of those fathers. I don't know why, but I just didn't feel a connection with Isaac at first. And it got worse. I reached a point where I knew I didn't want to be stuck in this kind of lifestyle, but I felt I had to because of responsibility. Those kinds of thoughts and emotions led me to want to take the easy way out of my marriage and family by simply "walking out," the coward's approach.

As Lindy told you, we didn't share this very dark period of our marriage at this point of our lives on YouTube or on social media. We were both trying to figure out what we wanted, and we needed privacy to do so. As daunting as it sounds, we did seriously consider separation, inevitably with the option of divorce after the separation period.

Lindy:

Even if you have been a longtime subscriber, you might be shocked to hear this from us. Behind our family vlogs—our supposed daily doses of happiness—we were deeply miserable. It wasn't our intention to create a fake reality. We were in denial ourselves. If you look carefully back to this time in our lives, you may notice that there was actually a period of time during which Tim was barely present in the videos. Before Isaac entered our lives, whenever we dined out, we would often see other couples eating in silence. We always promised each other that we would never let that happen. But there we were, our conversations had run dry and suddenly we had nothing to talk about. We couldn't even look at each other.

For over ten years, we had stuck together through thick and thin. In my wedding vows, I had called Tim my rainbow after the storm. He was there during my highest and lowest points, but there

I was, sitting in our apartment, home alone with our baby, staring at our wedding picture and wondering what had happened to us. We looked so happy and in love in the picture. When did we last look at each other like that? Where did the love go? This is the man I once adored the most in the world, and yet I couldn't find a single reason to like him at that moment. What happened to my husband? What happened to me?

We ran out of love for each other. To say we were at the brink of divorce would be an understatement. Nothing hurts more than hearing your husband tell you he doesn't love you the same anymore. We attempted marriage counseling, but the session was so hate filled that instead of finding ways to be more loving, we used it to vent our frustration and disappointment.

I was mentally prepared to start my life as a single parent and move back to the UK to be with my family and friends. I no longer wanted to be in our Hong Kong apartment. It was the very first home we had built together as a family, and we had shared so many wonderful memories there, but now it was tainted. It was filled only with memories of loneliness. I wanted to leave Hong Kong once and for all. I thought, as long as I left this miserable place, my misery would leave too. What I didn't realize was, you cannot escape from your problems by running away. No matter where you move, your problems will move with you. If I moved back to the UK, I would be surrounded by my family and loved ones again, but I would soon find out that my issues wouldn't magically disappear. I wasn't sure what Tim's plans would be on whether he would stay in Hong Kong or travel back and forth. Frankly, I didn't care.

After Isaac and I had flown back to Northern Ireland, I started looking at houses. After all, I couldn't stay at my parent's house forever. There was one house I went to see that felt different from all the others. It had a huge back garden, which would be perfect for my two dogs. The kitchen was large and spacious, something I didn't have in Hong Kong. Something about that house just made me feel safe and warm. With our family on the brink of splitting, this five-bedroom home would most likely not be the wisest choice. My mind told me to wait and think about it a little more, but something deep within told me this was where my son should grow up.

"I'll take it," I said to the site manager.

"Are you sure?" my elder sister asked cautiously.

"Yes, I'm sure." Alone or not, I was hopeful I could lead a happy life there.

In the midst of my pain over my family falling apart, I realized the only way to recover from the darkest days of my life was to lean on gratitude. I had already spent weeks feeling sorry for myself, yet that was getting me nowhere. Negative emotions only bred more fear and bitterness. I reminded myself each day that adversity was made to teach me important lessons and to strengthen my character. If I looked at my hardship as an opportunity for learning and growth, I knew I could come out of this experience faster, stronger, and more resilient. As numbing as my pain was, I made sure to remind myself that all this would eventually pass.

In the past, I had buried myself with work to keep my mind off my problems. It didn't help, as I was doing it with selfish intentions; there was nothing joyful or healing about it. During this time of turmoil, I was so desperate to find ways to fill the empty void in my heart that I even splurged on things I didn't need. Of course, that didn't help either. It was time to try something different.

During my darkest time, I had a moment in which I finally saw myself and my situation clearly. And I realized that the world was so much bigger than *my* problems. There were plenty of people in worse scenarios than mine. Yes, my marriage wasn't going well at all, but all the other aspects of my life weren't so bad. I still had plenty of things to be thankful for. I was healthy and young, and I still had so much more to give. Most of all, I had the most beautiful baby boy in the world. Isaac became my inspiration to remain strong.

Due to my failing marriage, I couldn't help but wonder if something was wrong with me. It's awful to admit it now, but it was almost as if I was depending on someone else to make me feel confident again. But I'd had enough of that. Instead of hoping for a miracle to show up in my life, I decided I should become one for someone else instead. I've always believed that I should teach what I learn. But at that point in my life, I decided I should start giving back in more meaningful ways.

Growing up, my beloved grandmother used to tell me how lucky I was to be able to go to school each day. She may be little in size, but my grandmother packs a mighty punch when it comes to her voice and her character. As I would sulk putting my socks on in the mornings before school, she frequently reminded me that she would've done anything as a child to be able to sit in a classroom and learn every day.

I've always looked at her as strong and invincible, but as I grew older, it became more apparent to me how limited her powers were because she could neither read nor write. As a child growing up in China, due to the war with Japan, my grandmother was unable to go to school, despite having a reputation as a very bright child. At the young age of five, her parents were brutally murdered in front of her eyes, then her fraternal grandmother had to sell her off to a family as a slave because she could no longer physically or financially take care of her.

My grandmother understood why she was forsaken, but because of this, she made it her life mission to be the best grandmother in the world. Eventually, my grandmother would meet a quiet but kind young man (my grandfather), and they would go on to create their little family together. She got her happy ending, but I will never forget how hard she'd had to work to create a life for herself after being abandoned and never having received a proper education.

Now as a young mother myself, I saw this inequality everywhere and felt my heart break for all the children in the world deprived of learning. Of course I want the very best for my child. Doesn't every mother? How can we truly make a difference in a child's life? In the end, it all comes down to one thing: education. After all, lack of education leads to sanitation and health issues, gender inequality, infrastructural challenges, lack of qualified teachers, familial economic instability, and many more issues. Education is truly the only way to a better future. As Nelson Mandela said, "No country can really develop unless its citizens are educated," yet 250 million children around the world would not even be able to read this sentence. It made my heart ache.

During this dark time in my life, when I was aching to change other people's lives, along with mine, I spent many nights tossing and turning in bed, frustrated by my limitations. I knew I really wanted to help educate children with few opportunities, but I didn't know where to start. I hoped to be able to build schools in underserved areas, but I knew without resources and contacts, I would go nowhere.

At that point, a wonderful man named Kenn had been my manager for about a year. Before Kenn, I had gone without management for a while because I took pride in my freedom, and thus did not want to be pressured into working with companies I did not believe in. But Kenn was different. Although he ran his company in Los Angeles, he actually resided in Cambodia. Isn't that crazy? Just like me, Kenn didn't like the complicated world and craved a more simple yet meaningful life. So he left Los Angeles and went to serve in the Peace Corps and volunteer as an English teacher. I admired his heart of gold and knew that if I wanted to work with anyone, it would be somebody with similar values. He had been giving me space, as he knew I was going through some issues, but one day he called to see how I was doing. I don't know why, but something told me that I could talk openly with him.

"Kenn, I want to build schools for underprivileged children. I can't explain why, but I've always somehow known that this is why my YouTube career took off. So I could do this."

"Great. Let's do it." No questions or anything. He was in. And those four words changed both our lives forever.

Mind you, unlike our usual projects and deals, this mission would not benefit Kenn at all. Yet he jumped at the opportunity. In fact, over the coming months and years, we would both end up emptying our pockets for this cause, but it was something I know we both did gladly.

As it turns out, at the time of our fateful phone call, Kenn had just recently finished reading a book called *The Promise of a Pencil: How an Ordinary Person Can Create Extraordinary Change*. The book is a compelling story told by Adam Braun, the founder of a nonprofit organization called Pencils of Promise. As of December 2016, that organization has served over thirty-five thousand students and 380 schools across the world. Amazing!

Kenn told me about the book, and we were both inspired to take a leap together to make a difference in the world. Since public relations is Kenn's forte, he did what he does best and started to plan how we could make building schools a reality. As you can guess, we have been working together with Pencils of Promise, or as I call them, my PoP family, ever since. It was as if everything happened at the right moment; it was all meant to be.

As Kenn did his thing, I also went back to my roots and started to do the one thing I'm good at: doodling. I designed a limited-edition shirt and decided to sell it, with the promise of donating whatever profit it generated to fund the building of a PoP school. I had spent the past year stressing about sustaining my family's livelihood in Hong Kong, but there I was, ready to squash that fear by giving away every penny.

Very quickly, my little idea exploded into full-color reality. I was overwhelmed by everybody's support for the cause. All these "strangers" I'd never met, from all around the globe, were now joining me on this mission to better the lives of children around the world. The less I focused on myself, the happier I became. I could smile again by making others smile. I realized that true fulfillment really does come from being able to serve others.

From that moment on, I felt I had found my purpose in life. I wanted to be part of something far bigger than myself. In the last two years, together with my "Bubscribers," we have built five schools with PoP so far in Laos and Ghana, and we don't plan to stop anytime soon. In these schools, over five hundred children, who might never have had the chance at an education, are being educated every day in a safe place. Being able to change other people's lives for the better ended up being a huge part of my recovery. When I was in need of a friend, I instead became a friend to someone else. Instead of being the one doing all the talking, I made myself listen. You receive what you give to others. You get back what you put out in the world. It was so simple, yet so powerful.

Throughout this remarkable awakening, and I can call it that because it really felt like I was finally waking up, even though I was gaining more self-love and power, I was still dealing with a lot of scars. It is easy to be happy for others when you are happy yourself. But when you're heartbroken inside, not so much. I was still in the process of healing, and it was neither easy nor fast.

The summer of 2014, just a couple of months after Tim and I had separated, that old wound was about to get ripped open again. Tim, who was still living in Hong Kong at the time, and I were invited to attend a good friend's wedding. We decided to go to Sheffield for the wedding, then drive down to London together to see our university friends afterward. We figured some time away might help our situation. Maybe a trip together would be just the thing.

Tim:

Let me tell you, my wife is truly an incredible person. You guys already know that because of her channel on YouTube, but in reality she is even more amazing. Somehow, through the depths of darkness, my wife managed to hang on to a glimmer of hope that our childhood love was still inside us. She still believed that we had not come to hate each other, but we had simply forgotten how to love each other. As a last-ditch effort to salvage our failing marriage, Lindy suggested that we take a few days out of our lives to truly be alone; no Isaac, no dogs, no work. Just the two of us. So after my best friend's wedding, we hitched a ride from Sheffield down to central London with a close friend.

Initially, I wasn't keen on the idea of spending time alone with my wife, as we had become a married couple who felt more like strangers in the past eight or nine months. I'll admit it: I was scared. As soon as I put on Facebook that I would be in London for a few days, my phone started to go off with people looking to meet up for dinner or a "few" drinks, to hang out. I was due to fly back to Hong Kong right after the trip, so I didn't have much time to see people. This obviously didn't bode well for our trip, because Lindy made it clear that she wanted to simply enjoy what would've been our last two days as a married couple before I went back to Hong Kong, not sit next to me while I got drunk with old university friends. At that point, we were planning on initiating the first steps of our separation after the trip.

Lindy:

I would be lying if I told you I wasn't worried about how I would handle my emotions at the wedding we were attending that weekend. Everything ended up going well until the ceremony. Watching our beautiful newlywed friends confess their love and promise to love and respect each other no matter what felt like a hundred daggers to my heart. It brought me back to our wedding vows and only reminded me of Tim's empty promises. Here I was celebrating somebody's marriage while mine was about to end. What did I do to deserve that pain? Why couldn't Tim have stepped up like a good husband and father like everyone else seemed to?

Long story short, our trip to London started out as a complete disaster. We were surrounded by beautiful rose gardens, but none of it mattered because we were both too focused on our anger.

One evening, rain started to fall as we stood on a street corner and started to fight. We were so wet and so angry, and just pouring all our frustration out at each other. It all came to a pivotal moment when I realized how stupid we both looked. I'd had enough. I had been trying to put broken pieces back together for so long, but the shards kept cutting me too deeply. Even if I managed to put the pieces back together, we would never be the same again. Feeling defeated, I wondered why I was fighting this battle that was doomed to fail. I looked at my husband, a person I couldn't even recognize anymore. I didn't want to bear the thought of Isaac growing up with divorced parents. But I was more scared at the thought of him growing up in an unhealthy family of resentful parents.

"Tim . . . let's just stop. I'm tired of fighting. We had a good run these twelve years. Let's face it, we've reached the end of our time together," I said weakly, tears mixing with the rain on my face.

"What are you saying?" my husband asked.

"We clearly don't bring out the best in each other anymore. I think it's time we put an end to this." I couldn't believe the words I was saying. We had discussed divorce many times in the past, but something about that day felt like it was really time to let go. He looked at me for a moment before nodding respectfully.

"You deserve someone much better," he said. He put his head down as he wept.

Suddenly, like magic, in that moment, all our hate, disappointment, resentment, and bitterness went away. That was the moment we both surrendered our selfishness, and suddenly, we were both able to breathe again. We no longer blamed each other. For the first time, we felt peaceful. It was over, but maybe we were all going to be okay after all.

After London, we had planned that I would fly back to Northern Ireland to sort out my new house, while Tim would fly back to Hong Kong to handle everything I had left behind. Since we still had a whole day left before parting ways, we decided to be civil.

"Let's just put everything aside and enjoy some time together as husband and wife for the last time," I suggested, fighting back my tears. For the first time in a while, he smiled at me.

For the rest of that day, we were the happiest we had been in a long time. We walked the streets of London, now able to appreciate the beautiful architecture surrounding us. I wanted to capture as many memories as possible, so I could cherish them. He ended up taking me to a musical, and it was so freeing to be able to laugh out loud again. After the show, we grabbed dinner and ice cream. You could say it was the perfect last date. We relaxed and cracked many jokes. It felt as if we were finally able to be us again.

The next day I dreaded. Since Tim's flight was later than mine, he walked me to my gate, and we said our goodbyes. It was in that moment that I realized just how much I had truly missed him. He kissed my forehead and turned away. I watched him walk off, begging silently for him to turn back around. But gradually, he faded into the crowds.

As it turns out, Tim felt the same way as I did. When he kissed my forehead, he realized how strained and tired I looked. As he walked away, he wanted to turn around to tell me he still loved me, but he was too filled with guilt. He didn't know how to face me. During the twelve-hour flight to Hong Kong, he cried the entire time, realizing how much of a fool he had been.

Tim:

I was in London, holding hands with someone who, for the last several months, I had pretty much hated. But after a few hours, we started to get comfortable with each other again. It was the feeling of finding something long lost, but very familiar, in your hands again. Little by little, feelings I could honestly say I hadn't felt for large parts of that year, started to return. Lo and behold, we ended up having two amazing days in London where we explored, watched a musical, ate, laughed . . . and more importantly, really let go of everything that had been clawing at us for the previous year. It was as if we had turned back time to when we had first dated as sixteen year olds: carefree, spontaneous, and young.

Sadly enough, the end of our trip would send us in opposite directions again. We were both due to leave from London's Heathrow Airport, with Lindy going back to Belfast and me returning to Hong Kong for work. Saying goodbye to Lindy and walking away from her in that airport was one of the hardest things I've ever had to deal with. It felt like a large and vital part of me had just been surgically removed. What I thought had been holding me back from living was actually what had kept me going all this time: my loving wife.

A feeling I had forgotten, a love that had been lost, a marriage and family I had nearly ruined. The penny dropped for me, walking through that airport to my flight. It felt like a massive wake-up call. I knew right then that what I was about to do would make me live in regret for the rest of my life. I was giving up too easily, just because things had gotten a little too tough.

I spent the entire twelve-hour flight back to Hong Kong in tears. I don't cry easily, so this was seriously the first time I had ever just lost it. I imagined what our lives would become, the family members disconnected, our work together falling apart, everything we had gone through for the last decade. . . . It all hit me like a huge slap on the face. From that moment onward, my life completely changed. I don't know if it was our trip to London that triggered it or the thought that I was about to lose my best friend for life. Regardless, I have never looked back since.

Lindy:

Tim confessed to me that he thought he was losing his wife but in truth, he was losing himself. Our time in London reminded him that I've been the same Lindy all along from twelve years ago. He promised to get his life back together and learn how to be a good husband and a caring father. Even though I was completely gratified by his words, I still had my doubts. The old me would've probably rebuked him with a sarcastic "Yeah, right." But this time, I only said two words: "Come home."

Since I had left Hong Kong so suddenly, it took Tim five weeks to sort out everything we had left behind before coming back to Northern Ireland. Those five weeks felt like our teenage years again. We had become used to being around each other all the time, so suddenly having distance between us made us cherish each other more. Of course, I was also nervous to have him back again. After all, our wounds were still in the process of healing. Sure, we'd had a great time on vacation in London, but how would things turn out when we got back to real life, with a house to maintain, work to manage, and most importantly, a baby to care for?

Once Tim finally returned to Belfast, we had a lot of work to do on ourselves. Slowly but surely, we rebuilt our marriage using trust, patience, and faith as the foundation. Our relationship will most likely never go back to how it used to be, but I can tell you that it's so much better now. We went through hell and back to get to where we are now. We fell in order to rise, and we have never looked back since. Our victory came from our complete surrender.

- Surrender from trying to control everything.
- Surrender from a blaming attitude.
- Surrender from expectations.
- Surrender from the past.

Tim and I both took responsibility for the downfall of our marriage. Instead of blaming, we decided to try understanding instead. It was not easy riding out the storm, but we learned a lot from our mistakes. Now our marriage is stronger than ever.

Tim also surrendered by finally embracing his new life as a father. Tim and Isaac are now inseparable. If you watch my vlogs, you will see how much Isaac adores his father. I am able write this book every day thanks to my amazing husband being so hands-on with our son. As I type this, I can hear them both giggling downstairs.

Tim:

You don't overcome something so profoundly damaging overnight. Since that London trip, and up to and including this day, Lindy and I work daily on our marriage. I used to think that being married was the final step a couple could take (in terms of being in a relationship), and that marriage would "seal" us together forever. But through everything I've experienced since being married, my view on that has changed.

A marriage doesn't guarantee you will be together forever; at the end of the day, it's only a piece of paper. It takes love, respect, trust, understanding, and faith in your relationship to make it last. Don't get me wrong; there are still days when Lindy and I are at each other's throats. We still have our fair share of quarrels and disagreements. But what's changed is that with everything we've been through, we have learned that instead of focusing on each other's flaws or inadequacies (because we all know it's easier to blame and shame rather than change ourselves), we focus on each other's positive attributes.

I can't say I don't drink anymore, because that would be an outright lie, but I do so now in a much more responsible manner. The fact is, I don't miss the old me anymore. Everyone has to grow up eventually. The darkest year of my life, the one in which I almost lost my wife and son, maybe forever, was also one of the most important years of my life. It was the year I transitioned from being a boy into a man.

One last thing: I do have to give huge credit to my loving wife, who has stuck by me, put up with me throughout all these years, and made me who I am today. All the things you see on our YouTube channel, those comments on how I am a "good" dad—none of that would have ever been possible without a loving and understanding wife showing me the way. If I could share one cliché quote with you guys, it would be this: "Be with someone who brings out the best in you." So thank you, Lindy Gei Yan Tsang, for bringing the best version of me out. I love you.

Lindy:

That very house where I sensed I might end up raising my son on my own ended up being the happy home we all live in today. Scarred from the experience of having our first child, I expressed to Tim that I didn't think I'd ever want another child. I loved my husband so much that I didn't want to risk our marriage being in shambles again. Tim nodded. He understood and respected my choice. But here I am, twenty weeks pregnant, our second baby on the way. You see, you just never know how life will turn out. I didn't think I would ever be happy again, and now I'm the happiest I think I've ever been.

I can see how much Tim has grown and changed over the years. Alcohol no longer controls him the way it used to. What I came to realize was that I couldn't force my husband to change; only he can change himself. I can only focus on myself and work on changing my attitude and becoming more patient and understanding. This shared attitude, that we were both to blame and that it was both of our responsibilities to change, saved our marriage.

Tim and I nearly failed when we demanded that the other was supposed to bring us happiness. Why did we almost fail? Because only we are responsible for our happiness, after all. This isn't Hollywood. This is real life. It takes no effort to fall in love, but it takes hard work to stay in love. Let our story be a reminder that relationships aren't meant to be rainbows and butterflies all the way. Relationships can be incredibly painful and hard. Love isn't a feeling but rather a choice. You choose to stay in love despite your loved one's shortcomings and all your differences. A great love isn't about having a pain-free "perfect" fairy tale relationship; it is about being able to overcome hardship together.

My life could have gone down a completely different path. I could've remained bitter and continued to place blame on my husband for everything wrong in my life. Our marriage could've ended in shambles. Instead of letting my adversity defeat me, I have used it as an advantage to sculpt me into a better person. I truly believe I have become more patient, kind, loving, and understanding from it. I certainly surprised myself by realizing that I am actually much stronger than I ever imagined. Most of all, I came out on the other side, happier than ever. I started as the victim but came out in victory. Don't be surprised if you end up surprising yourself. Our rough patches in life teach us the most, and I am truly grateful for them. Experience truly is the ultimate teacher.

Last year, I was fortunate enough to go on a field trip to visit one of the schools the Bubscribers and I funded together for the children of Laos. As we traveled in our SUV to the village high up in the mountains, I saw children happily trekking uphill to go to school with no shoes on . . . with big smiles on their faces. I couldn't help but wonder: Did they do this every single day, walk up a mountain without shoes?

Once we arrived on the school grounds, we were told not to distract the students while they were studying. As I discreetly observed the children through the window, I noticed their smiles were even bigger inside the classroom. I had never seen this degree of happiness in a classroom before. Where I come from, things are very different. It's easy to take our education for granted—I know I have. We complained about having to wake up early, about being bored in class, and about the annoyance of homework. Instead of wanting to be somewhere else, these children were genuinely delighted to be in school, thrilled to have been given the opportunity to learn every single day.

After spending some time getting to know the children, I was ready for lunch. As we sat and enjoyed the lovely lunch prepared for us by the school members, I watched the children in the field. They were all playing together with one very deflated ball, but laughing, smiling, and enjoying their game.

As I was eating my lunch—sticky rice, which the Lao enjoy as it keeps them fuller for longer—a stray dog approached me under the table. Heartbroken by how undernourished she appeared, I started to offer her some of my food. Immediately, I noticed two school members looking at each other in concern. My manager gently leaned over to tell me that while what I did was in good intention, it could be construed as insulting to the people there. They already didn't have much to eat, yet there I was, throwing my food under the table. I immediately apologized for my ignorance, even as I felt sorry for the dog. I had never considered that the simple lunch we were eating was actually considered a feast for the villagers in that mountain. I felt so ashamed at my ignorance.

After lunch, the team took us for a walk to explore the village. I saw two children, maybe around four or five years old, playing with sticks on the floor, as if it were the best game in the world. There was no electricity or clean water up in the mountain, so the villagers often drink from the very same river where people do their washing. I was told it was common for an average family of twelve to share a small plate of greens with two fish about the size of sardines. I can't imagine myself being full eating two sardines, never mind having to share that meal between eleven others. I fell silent, feeling humbled and a bit sad.

But despite their simple living conditions, I have never seen so much joy as I did that day, among those broken shacks. It was so uplifting to experience the positive spirit from the villagers. That day, I got to meet some of the happiest people I'd ever met in my life, and guess what? They don't have much in the way of worldly possessions at all. Those children taught me that you can always find a reason to be grateful. As I returned to my comfortable accommodations that night, I realized again just how blessed I truly was. My life has never been the same since.

Bubz's Rules

- Only in darkness can true glory be revealed. In every trial, there is a treasure. There is an opportunity for you to grow stronger. There are lessons to be learned. There is a stronger and better you on the other side.

- When you need happiness the most, provide it for someone else. You will be surprised to know that, like a boomerang, happiness will always come back to you. True joy comes from being able to serve others.

- The world is bigger than our problems. Someone always has it worse. Don't let your negative emotions take away your ability to see the world clearly. There is always something to be thankful for. Even after battling each day, be grateful for making it through yet another alive. As long as there is tomorrow, there is an opportunity to love, learn, and laugh.

- Whatever you are feeling right now, it will pass. Better days are ahead, I promise. The past does not equal the future. Sometimes in life, things need to get worse before they get better. Always be hopeful.

- Victory and happiness come from surrendering. Surrender yourself from victimizing, hatred, blaming, making excuses, expecting, trying to control everything, and the need to be right.

- Yes, you will meet lots of imperfect people along the way. You, too, are imperfect. I believe that the ones that hurt us the most can also teach us the most. Compassion goes a long way. You can never truly recover with hatred in your heart.

Blissful Living

I f you haven't realized it yet, everything we've covered in this book so far, including learning to be the master of your thoughts, nurturing a beautiful heart, and embracing your individuality, all goes down to the very same goal: to be happy.

Everything we aim to do or achieve in life should be working toward the very same goal. We just want to be happy. And why wouldn't we want to be happy? It's scientifically proven that happy people live longer, healthier lives and build better relationships.

Here's the question: Why are there so many miserable people on Earth today? After all, our lifestyles are better than ever. There's a good chance that if you're reading this book, you're not dealing with drought, famine, or war right now (though of course, sadly, so many people still are). However, it seems like the more we own, the more depressed we feel. Advanced telecommunications have made us better "connected" than ever, and yet we have never felt lonelier. In this superficial and materialistic day and age, how can we be truly joyful from within?

Like most people out there, I once believed that I could only be happy for a reason. I lived with this misconception for many years, and yet it didn't occur to me that happiness is so simple that we often miss it.

This chapter will explore the simplicity of true joy. Together, we will unlock the final elements to blissful living. I have tried to give you all my secrets and knowledge about how to become the best that you can be for yourself and others. Now as we near the end of this book, let's dive deeper and explore how to live the best kind of life for yourself. Because you know in your heart that you deserve it.

Stop Living like You'll Live Forever

We live in a stress-filled world, and it's so easy to get caught up in the chaos of life itself. Is it me, or has being busy suddenly become the new norm? In fact, apparently the busier you are, the more "important" you are. Competitive and frightened, we're in such a hurry, rushing to get from place to place to get things done, that we are missing out on life. As the line in the John Lennon song goes, "Life is what happens to us while we're busy making other plans."

We get so caught up with growing up that we forget our parents, grandparents, and loved ones are growing old. I am deeply regretful with how I handled the first six months of my son's life. Without giving myself maternity leave, I was so busy trying to balance my career and a newborn simultaneously that I only remember being frustrated most of the time. I never got to truly relax and enjoy my baby, and I'll never get to relive those moments.

I try to hold zero regrets in my life, because I know that harboring regret is useless, but I know Isaac deserved more of my undivided attention then, and it pains me I wasn't able to give that to him. I can only learn from my mistakes and make up for it by striving to be more present than ever now. But I'll never get his first year back. No matter what you choose to do in life, know that time does not wait for you.

There is a quote making the rounds on the Internet that people have attributed to the Dalai Lama, though I'm not sure anyone has proven it was actually him who said this. Regardless of who said it, though, I love its sentiment. When asked what surprised him the most about humanity, here is his response:

"Man. Because he sacrifices his health in order to make money. Then he sacrifices money to recuperate his health. And then he is so anxious about the future that he does not enjoy the present; the result being that he does not live in the present or the future; he lives as if he is never going to die, and then dies having never really lived." -Dalai Lama

When I first read these words, they shook me to my very core; they have honestly changed my way of living. Nobody likes to think about death because it's morbid and makes us uncomfortable. But let's not fool ourselves; our days on Earth are numbered. (Sorry if this has suddenly gotten a bit depressing, but I promise it's all for good reason.)

As you already know, I lost my grandfather to lung cancer several years ago. The thing was, he never paid attention to his lungs until the day he was told by the doctor that his lungs were in trouble. Suddenly, knowing the number of days he had left on Earth had been cut short made him wish he had lived his life differently. But by the time he found out, it was too late. My grandfather's story makes me think a lot about life itself. It makes me sad to know that most people only realize what truly matters near the end of their lives. It doesn't have to be this way. If they had realized sooner, imagine how different their lives could have been—potentially more peaceful, fulfilled, and meaningful.

We already know life is short, yet we act like we're going to live forever. We obsess about "securing" ourselves for the future, when the truth is, we could be gone tomorrow. When we're in the final days of our lives (I'll lighten things up soon, I promise), we're not going to ask to see our bank accounts or to hug our university degrees. What will matter the most then will be the people by our side. So if our relationships end up mattering the most, why shouldn't they matter the most right now? Time is slipping away as you're reading, and you will never, ever get these seconds back. So why aren't we living in balance?

Don't get me wrong; I'm not saying it's bad to concentrate on your career. It's important to have goals, dreams, and a purpose. Obviously, we all need jobs for a reason, because that's how we pay the bills and feed ourselves. I've admitted I can be a bit of a workaholic myself, because I thrive when I know I'm being productive, but it's important to live in balance. Your happiness and well-being are important. Living in balance shouldn't be a choice or something you put in the back seat until something drastic happens.

You've probably heard the saying "too much of anything is bad for you," and it's completely true. For example, you can strive to be the best that you can be, but if you drive yourself to perfectionism, you may end up hurting yourself and those around you.

As you know, since my parents had to work full-time, my grandparents brought me up. Now I'm so thankful for the fact that my mother-in-law takes care of Isaac two days a week. You have no idea how much stuff I can get done in the space of two days, and it gives Tim and me a chance to have some quality time together. Well, my grandparents had four grandchildren, seven days a week, twenty-four hours a day. My grandmother's bedroom was like a pigsty, because we all slept in the same room. As crazy as we were, I don't remember a single day when they complained about having us.

As a child, I promised myself that I would take care of them when I was older. My granddad passed away before I had the opportunity, so I made sure I wouldn't miss the chance with my grandmother. The problem was, I ended up getting too carried away with making a living, and now she is growing older by the day. I could buy her things, and she would appreciate every little gesture, but what she wants the most is me, of course. Sometimes, when I would give her allowance and gifts, she would huff at me, and I couldn't understand why. Didn't she know that I was simply busy?

As you guys know, as I write these pages, I am currently five months pregnant. So as you can imagine, I'm on a time crunch to finish this book and things have been pretty crazy. But I also want to concentrate as much time toward my family as possible, so that I am making the most out of whatever time I have left before my second child arrives. After taking a much needed two-week break from writing to spend time with my family in Hong Kong, I only got back to Northern Ireland two days ago. Since it had been a while since I last wrote, I struggled to get my brain moving again. I also knew that I only have a few days left until my husband and son join me from Hong Kong, so I had to squeeze as much writing in as possible before I start to juggle work and family life again.

Yet two full days passed, and I barely had two pages of quality writing. I was feeling frustrated and overwhelmed with the endless list of things waiting to be done that week, when I got a text from my aunty asking me to call my grandmother. I had been out of the country for two weeks, and I had no idea my grandmother had been worrying about me and waiting for my phone call. She knew I had to fly a long-haul flight while being pregnant, and she was anxious about me being home alone, primarily worried that I wasn't feeding myself properly. Isn't it crazy how I am a full-grown adult, and yet I will always be a little child to my beloved grandmother?

Despite being bombarded with work, I decided to visit my grandmother. It was a beautiful, sunny day, so I took her grocery shopping, and then we spent the afternoon watching TV while having some tea. She told me she missed me a lot and wished I lived closer so she could see me more. As happy as it made me to know that she'd had such a great day, my heart broke a little. My grandmother doesn't need me to earn big bucks for her. Her love doesn't cost anything. Nothing could make my grandmother happier than seeing me indulge in some of her delicious meals. I ended up going home with a huge bag of frozen meals and a pile of fruit. I made a promise to her that she would only see me more and more from here on. Giving my grandma my time is more valuable than anything else I could do for her.

Time, rather than money, is actually the most valuable currency in the world. Luckily, we are all given the same number of hours in a day as everyone else. I go to bed each night so grateful for each day I have been given. The fact that I know my days on this Earth are numbered inspires me to enjoy every moment I have on it. The beauty of life is that we're not meant to last forever, which should drive us to live each day with meaning and purpose.

It's Not about the Money, Money, Money . . .

Like a lot of people, many think that if they won the lottery, life's problems would all disappear. Do you know that every time they have conducted a study on a group of lottery winners, they have discovered one truth? As ecstatic as they were at the beginning, most lottery winners returned back to the same level of happiness they were at before they won.

Now I have also won the lottery myself – I believe it was £10—but I'm not sure that quite counts. However, I do think I can understand something about these lottery winners. When I used to work for my parent's restaurant, I received a humble weekly wage. Even though it wasn't a lot, it was more than enough for me to do all the things that made me happy. You can imagine my excitement when my YouTube hobby was unexpectedly able to generate income that not only outgrew my restaurant wages but actually doubled and tripled them. I was thrilled because it meant I could save more money to do more of the things I like. That excitement eventually faded as I got used to receiving that amount each week.

Throughout the years, as my YouTube career took off, I earned more, but I also expected more. In fact, it no longer became special to me. I felt like I needed certain numbers on my revenue report in order for me to know that I was progressing in my career. Isn't that crazy?

It is said that the lower your expectations, the higher your happiness. I wonder if this is the reason the happiest people in the world are those who don't have a lot in terms of material possessions, like those smiling schoolchildren in Laos. I am a realist—I'm not saying you shouldn't have any expectations at all. The key is to live life striving to do the best you can while being able to manage your expectations. How? By always keeping a grateful attitude.

Going back to my experience, I warn you: I'm about to sound like an ungrateful jerk here. Maybe my "success" grew too fast, but even as my income went up, my happiness was plummeting. When I first started out on YouTube, my focus was to share my knowledge with the beauty community. I loved doing what I was doing, and I was more than happy doing it all for free. Suddenly, when I started to be able to make a living from it, as much as I tried to not let the business side affect me, it did.

Around that time, my then-manager said something that made me anxious for an entire year. He told me, "If you're not growing, you're dying." From that point on, I felt fearful, and I became obsessed with staying on top of the game. As in all jobs, there were a bunch of things that were completely out of my control, yet I made myself believe that I could control everything. I obsessed about my numbers, from my subscribers to my view count to my monthly revenue. All I knew was, I needed those numbers to hit certain targets for me to confirm that my channel was not "dying." I was obsessed about having stability, yet I was becoming emotionally unstable myself. I became a slave to my expectations, then constantly felt defeated and exhausted trying to chase it in this never-ending battle. Your happiness and expectations are tied together like seats on a seesaw. When expectations go up, happiness goes down.

You have to understand that there is a difference between goals and expectations. You can set goals as high as you want, and you should work hard to achieve your dreams and aspirations. But you also must try to do the best you can while also letting go of your expectations of what the outcome should be. The biggest lie we tell ourselves is that life is supposed to go a certain way. There are too many things in this world that are out of our control; having high expectations won't help us along the way.

I definitely learned this lesson the hard way. As my channel was really taking off, and I was growing and earning at my peak, I was mentally and physically drained. Soon enough, I forgot why I had started a YouTube channel in the first place. The joy in doing what I did was gone, and so I began to lose myself.

I know I should have been grateful for everything that happened at that time, and in many respects, I was. But at the same time, I felt empty, and I couldn't understand why. I was becoming successful, yet I couldn't enjoy life because I was too busy being stressed and anxious, worrying how to maintain it all. Tim and my friends had also started to get frustrated, as I was no longer making time for them anymore. YouTube started to consume every part of my life, and for the first time, I lost perspective of what really matters. True fulfillment comes from being able to serve others, and because I was always thinking only of myself, I became miserable.

After various breakdowns, I realized that this system was clearly not working for me anymore. After all, nothing is more important than my well-being, inner peace, and sense of happiness. So, I made a decision to stop obsessing about my numbers and to focus on learning and doing what I loved instead.

Today, I have no idea the exact number of subscribers I have. All I know is that I am grateful for each and every single one. I no longer put so much pressure on myself to create content. It's been almost a decade since I started, and I still love what I do because I am still learning every single day. Being able to learn, inspire, and experience all these amazing things in my life will always be my biggest reward. But I want to be sure I continue to enjoy what I do, so if inspiration doesn't come, I'm not going to be hard on myself. I trust my intuition that in time, it will come to me if it's meant to be.

Once I finally figured out how to take the focus off myself, I put my focus back on enriching the lives of others. I started by focusing on some simple things: putting smiles on people's faces and making people realize their beauty. Now I'm determined to keep building schools for underprivileged children around the world, and I don't plan on stopping there. Even though now I don't earn as much as I used to, I feel richer than ever, because I have meaning in my life again.

When I first started my channel, I was still very young, so under-standably, I probably had more selfish intentions inside than even I realized. A lot of what I thought would make me happy actually ended up consuming me. I realized what so many before me have realized—that money and fame, no matter how big or small, could only give me temporary happiness. I know far too many people with more success and money than I could ever have dreamed of, who probably don't have half the happiness I've found in my life.

Even though money can be the answer to a lot of problems, it turns out that it doesn't always guarantee happiness, at least not long-term happiness anyway. What I have learned is that true joy isn't dependent on getting what you want. You already know this from reading all the stories of rich people's lives getting derailed despite the luxurious living.

What you'll discover is that the more you give, the more you receive. When you are finally able to step outside of yourself to help others, that will give you the most meaning. I finally learned that true fulfillment comes from being part of something that's bigger than you.

Like I said, I don't think you have to build orphanages and schools to help someone. You can start by looking around you. Just give more of yourself by offering your time to help your friends, family, neighbors, or community. As I mentioned already, spending time with my awesome little grandmother makes me ever so joyful. Each and every one of us are drawn to different causes. The gist is, as long as you serve a purpose that's larger than yourself, you will have more meaning and joy in your life.

Now I am happy to say that I live in balance. My life is much more relaxed, peaceful, and meaningful. If your life enables you to pay the bills, treat yourself a little every so often, and leaves you some time to spend with your loved ones, you are already living a rich life.

If your job doesn't fulfill you emotionally, know that you can also find bliss by doing what you love outside of work. Maybe you love to paint, dance, or read. Life isn't about living excessively but about living in balance.

I always believe that as long as there is a will, there is a way. If you are deeply unsatisfied with your job, know that it is possible to make a change in your life. You may have to take a few steps back, but you could also gain miles in return. The accomplishments that mean the most to me are the ones I know I put blood, sweat, and tears into. The road to your dreams can be difficult, but who said it was always going to be easy? All dreams require sacrifice. The easier way isn't always the better way.

If You're Not in the Job You Love, Love the Job You're In

Maybe for now, you still don't want to make any drastic changes to your lifestyle. In this case, never underestimate your worth based on what you do for a living. I read a story about a man who spent years being disappointed with his profession of being a garbage man. In comparison to his friends, his job seemed so dull and unglamorous. Still, he had to keep that job in order to pay the bills and feed his family. He had been in this profession for several years and without any other qualifications, and he honestly didn't know what other field he could move into. In the meantime, he made a choice that if he was going to stay in that job, he was going to be the best garbage man there ever was. Since he wasn't in the job he loved, he was going to love the job he was in.

His mission led him to look at his job differently. While he used to just do his thing day in and out, punching the clock, he started to put more effort and thought by wheeling garbage cans straight into the resident's driveways. He had always had a strong desire to serve others, and this was his small way of making a difference. He smiled, conversed with people, and offered help as often as he could. Soon enough, he built a reputation of being the friendliest garbage man in town. In time, his satisfaction improved, and he came to love his job. It isn't your profession that defines your feeling of purpose and happiness; it's your perspective.

"Success is not the key to happiness. Happiness is the key to success. If you love what you are doing, you will be successful." -Albert Schweitzer

Money Is Not Evil

Of course, let's not deny that we live in a world today that's fueled by money. It's difficult to go through a single day without thinking about it. That's why we have jobs in the first place. We need it to pay bills and to clothe and feed ourselves and our families. Money can be a wonderful thing, because it allows us to do things we enjoy, like going to the cinema and dining out. It can be used to fund amazing causes and research to change lives for the better. It can make the impossible possible, yet at the same time, it can also cause destruction.

There is a misconception that money is evil, but the truth is, it's not. Our relationship with money is a different story. It's when you worship money that it becomes a problem. You see, I know too well that money can blind you and make you lose perspective. People can worry and obsess so much over money that they will fight, lie, steal, and even kill to get it. What's most ironic is that money is supposed to make us feel more secure, yet it often ends up controlling us. Some of the grumpiest and stingiest people I know are the ones who have the most.

There is nothing wrong with being successful. I am so incredibly proud of all my driven friends who are passionate about their career and goals. You just have be careful not to let money control you.

Maybe for some of you, you are scraping to get by. I can sympathize and know it must be tough. Can I gently remind you that making yourself worried sick about it won't make the situation any better? It takes up a lot of energy, but it doesn't get us anywhere.

Let me remind you one more time: We cannot control our situations. The one thing we can control is our attitude. It's a lot easier said than done, but remember, many of the happiest people in the world today are the ones who don't have a lot. On the contrary, many of the loneliest are the richest. Know that your joy doesn't have to be tied up in accumulating great wealth.

Money is supposed to be part of your life, but it doesn't have to become your world. Instead of murmuring and complaining, focus on the solution while maintaining a positive attitude. Plan and spend wisely so you can pay for the necessities of life while appreciating the little joys in life. Don't be fooled into comparing your wealth and possessions with others.

Society often tries to tell us we cannot be happy unless we have this or that when, truth is, if you have a roof over your head, food in your fridge, and a place to sleep at night, you are already richer than the majority of the world. If you woke up this morning healthy and happy, you are more blessed than the one million people who will not survive this week. If you can read these words right now, you are more fortunate than the three billion people who cannot read at all.

You know how some nights, you'll raid your kitchen cabinets because you're peckish and looking for a bite, yet you cannot find anything you want to eat? First-world problem, right? Well, millions of people on this Earth today don't even know when their next meal will be. My intention is not to make you feel guilty, but to help you gain perspective. You can always find a reason to be grateful.

> *"Too many people spend money they haven't earned to buy things they don't want to impress people they don't like." -Will Rogers*

- *You can buy a beautiful mansion, but not a home.*
- *You can buy companions, but not friends.*
- *You can buy sex, but not love.*
- *You can buy all the medicine in the world, but not health.*
- *You can buy an antique clock, but not time.*

You actually have everything you'll ever need to be joyful. Society doesn't seem to want us to realize this, but we actually don't need a lot to get by. I refuse to be defined by what I have. I would rather be known as someone who respects others, not as someone who owns nice things. I will leave this Earth the very same way as I entered it, with nothing. Regardless of what you believe, you cannot take money to your grave. It's possible to work, live, and love without worrying about all the material things. I don't say any of this lightly; I know how incredibly lucky I am. But I truly believe that the happiness I've found would not disappear if my career fizzled overnight. My hard-earned sense of self-worth is bigger than my bank account, and it always will be. I hope yours is too.

- *Work to drive passion and to pay the bills.*
- *Live life grateful.*
- *Love everyday.*

My cousin worked as a successful accountant for many years. Even though everything looked great on the surface, he was miserable on the inside. It turns out that he hated his profession. When he reached his mid-thirties, he realized that time was ticking. If he wanted to make a change for himself, it had to be now or never. He had hated his job for over a decade and only stayed because it paid well and made his parents happy. Deep within, because of that, he felt resentment for his parents, so it strained their relationship for many years. One day, he finally stopped to ask himself one vital question: What was the point of overworking himself to that extent, to be constantly stressed and defeated, in order to earn all that cash he couldn't even enjoy because he was too busy and unhappy to appreciate it?

My cousin looked at the mirror and saw what his lifestyle was doing to him. Due to stress, he had accumulated a load of weight, his skin was covered in acne, and his hair had even started to fall out at the back of his head.

Since he was the only child, his parents had always placed great pressure on him. But as much as he tried to be their obedient son, he could not live that life anymore. It was all a lie. He decided his well-being and happiness should come first, so he quit his job and traveled to Asia to teach English. Unfortunately, his parents could not understand his choice, so they fell out for a period of time.

It was not his parent's intention to make things difficult for him. They just thought stability would result in happiness for their son. But sometimes, what you think is best doesn't always end up being what's best for others. I am sure many of you out there can relate to this (my hand is up too). But his parents eventually accepted that their happiness should come from their son's happiness and not the other way around. When they saw how much happier and healthier he had become in his new life, they understood his choice. His salary may have decreased, but his happiness increased many times over. For him, he had to lose a little to gain a lot in return. Now, he is living a "rich" life, and since he is happier, all his relationships have improved, including with his parents.

Find Your Purpose

"The two most important days in your life are the day you are born and the day you find out why." -Unknown

Many people think their purpose is in their profession, but it's actually a lot simpler than that. Having purpose is when you're able to do what's meaningful to *you*. It comes from knowing what your gift is and being able to share it with the world. A meaningful life is not about being wealthy, popular, or having status, it's about being able to live authentic and grateful lives, knowing what our talents and gifts are, while being able to share them with others.

Like most people, you might be sighing right now, saying, "I have no idea what my purpose is." Don't worry; you are not alone. It's okay to feel a little frustration. If you struggle with figuring out what your drive is, then figure out what your passion is instead. What can you spend hours and hours immersing yourself into? What do you care the most about? What makes your heart sing? I promise you that your passion will lead you straight to your purpose.

It's proven that people who are committed to whatever gives their life meaning live much happier lives. It's said that our purpose is like the roof of a home filled with happiness. Purpose acts like a shield, preventing unhappiness from leaking into our lives. Find your purpose and protect it.

Some people would say their purpose is to be a great teacher, parent, photographer, or musician. Your purpose could be absolutely anything. I believe my grandmother's purpose is to make sure her grandchildren never experience hunger. I know my purpose is to inspire and share love and happiness wherever I go so people around me can live the best life possible. If you are unsure what you're passionate about, I encourage you to open up your horizons by trying new things. Inspiration is actually all around us; we just have to go and look for it.

Can't we all agree that being inspired is the most blissful feeling in the world? Bliss is when you're so wrapped up in what you're doing that even if it is work, it doesn't feel like it. They say if you love what you do, you won't work a single day of your life. We already know that following your bliss isn't always going to be easy, but inspiration will give you the courage to do whatever gives you meaning, thus allowing you to live in the moment. When you are inspired by purpose, you don't know where you're headed. But just follow that light, and it will take you where you need to be. Stay inspired.

It's been an incredible journey writing this book, but it hasn't always been easy. I procrastinated for months as I wasn't sure where to begin. Still, there were many moments when I didn't know where I was going, and yet I just knew I had to take it one page at a time. When I couldn't find inspiration, rather than waiting for it to magically come to me, I went out to look for it. Before I knew it, here I am, nearly at the end of this book. Chasing your passion is very much like writing a book: You just have to start writing, taking it one page at a time.

Going Nowhere? Think Again

I remember it used to take days for a handwritten letter to arrive at my childhood friend's house in the mail. Not even that, but it required me to physically leave my house and search for a post office or a mailbox. Now, if I want to contact her, I just need to pick up my phone and send her a quick text. In fact, I don't even need to type anything; I could just send an emoji. If I want a buy a new vase for my dining room, I don't even have to leave the comfort of my home. I can browse thousands of choices online and have it delivered straight to my door tomorrow. Why would I want to go tackle the crazy crowds for the post-holiday sales when I could just sit with my feet up, with a glass of wine and my laptop in hand?

In today's fast-paced world, we have been conditioned and spoiled with convenience because we are always in a hurry. We get discouraged when we don't get our way or when results aren't attained immediately. Do you feel like everyone is always running around while you are left behind, feeling defeated and confused? I've been there.

Take a nice, deep breath with me. Remember what we said about comparing ourselves to others, and that we're all different for a reason? Of course there will be some younger people who gain success, but that early success does not always equal a happy life. Some might marry in their early twenties but wind up divorcing a few years later, while others may not find love until their forties but are tied up for life. Some might start a successful company in their mid-twenties, only to have it crash and burn a year later, whereas others don't find success until they are fifty.

Since life is not a race, we are all supposed to be moving at our own paces. Stop focusing on other people's journeys and focus on your path. Use your energy to focus on building your character and skills. Let me share something about an amazing man named Jack Ma.

Jack Ma is the founder of the Alibaba Group, one of the Internet's largest companies. It dominates a whopping 80 percent of China's online e-commerce. Its sales in 2013 were estimated at $240 billion, which is more than Amazon and eBay's sales total put together. Yet did you know he was rejected numerous times before he became China's richest and most successful person?

As a teenager, Jack Ma applied to college both in China and abroad over a dozen times and was rejected every time. After failing the national university entrance exam in China three times, he was accepted at a teacher's school. Yes, what's amazing about Jack Ma is that before he launched one of the most successful companies in the world, he used to work as an English teacher. In fact, he was the only teacher assigned to five hundred students, yet he received less than $15 each month. Do you know how he learned English to begin with? He used to offer his services for free as a guide to tourists for eight whole years, and he conversed with them enough to develop the language.

Freshly out of college, he applied for many jobs and got rejected by them all, including by Kentucky Fried Chicken. But just because you have a bad start does not mean you won't have a good finish. His career started out full of failures, and even when he started Alibaba in 1999, he persevered when the company didn't perform well. Now his company has 450 million customers.

"Many years ago, I wanted to change the world. Now I think if I want to change the world, we change ourselves. Changing ourselves is more important and easier than changing the world." -Jack Ma

Jack Ma wanted to improve the world, so he improved himself first: not only his talents but as an entire person overall. He knew that if he respected and took care of his team, they would take care of his customers. As smart and talented as you are, nobody wants to work for or with a rude, condescending person. Your talents come hand in hand with your character. If you can focus your life on empowering others, you will be empowered in the process.

Here are more examples of people who found their calling a bit late:

- Alan Rickman, after an acting career spent mostly on stage, didn't land his first major movie role until he was 42. Morgan Freeman, who followed a similar path, didn't land his first major movie role until 52.
- Legendary fashion designer Vera Wang designed her first dress at forty.
- Henry Ford created the revolutionary Model T car when he was 45.
- Stan Lee created the legendary Marvel Universe in his forties.

Your destiny is not to be the same as everyone else. Everyone is meant to walk their own path, so cherish and enjoy your journey.

Even if today is hard and things don't get better in a week, month, or a year, take heart and don't give up.

Live in the Moment

"Few of us ever live in the present. We are forever anticipating what is to come or remembering what has gone." -Louis L'Amour

It's a shame that many of us miss the opportunity to be happy because we live with an "I'll be happy when . . ." attitude.

- "I'll be happy when my exams are over."
- "I'll be happy when I find a job."
- "I'll be happy when I get a pay raise."
- "I'll be happy when I get an apartment."
- "I'll be happy when I get a house."
- "I'll be happy when I find my soulmate."
- "I'll be happy when people stop pissing me off."
- "I'll be happy when I win the lottery."

You get the gist. The list goes on.

Happiness can only be now, because it is the only time that truly exists. Whenever I'm having a bad day, I feel a sense of reassurance knowing that the sun will rise again tomorrow for another new day. Tomorrow will always come, but you'll never get today again, so why not live in the moment? Don't wait for the future to be happy because, guess what? You actually don't have control over the future.

Many of us let our troubled pasts and our future worries overshadow our present moments so much that we end up frustrated and anxious. The fact is, you and I can't guarantee that we will still be here tomorrow. The only time that truly exists is now. *Now* is the only thing we have any control over.

While some people are too busy looking into the sky and waiting for the future to come, others are too busy looking back. These people believe the past is more powerful than the present, but the fact is that it's pointless to get stuck in a moment of your life that's in the past and cannot be changed. It's natural to feel frustration, anger, and sadness, but when you refuse to come to terms with the past and move on with your life, you end up being the very one responsible for your unhappiness. No amount of guilt can amend the past and no amount of anxiety can change the future.

Instead of focusing on the past and future, focus on the "now," because you actually have to deal with the present to get to where you want to be. Don't let yesterday or tomorrow ruin today, because you will never get this moment back. Learn from the past, be prepared for the future, and live in the present. Your future has no room for the past.

Believe it or not, happiness is actually up to you. Have you ever heard the phrase "pursuit of happiness"? The United States Constitution grants it as one of our inalienable rights as humans. But while some pursue happiness, others create it.

When you are truly joyful, you exude positivity. Don't you want to wake up each day excited to be on this adventure called life? We learn best when we teach something, so teach the world what happiness is about, and you'll learn something about yourself in the process.

Keep Calm and Stress Less

While I can say I'm pretty good at being a positive person, my biggest struggle has always been my struggle with stress. Like a lot of you, I am very prone to it. I am naturally proactive, and I flourish in productivity, so I crave that feeling of satisfaction when errands are completed, deadlines are hit, and goals are reached. But while I often live life at one hundred miles per hour, sometimes I don't know how to stop. Then it doesn't matter how well I'm doing, because eventually I burn out and crash. As I've said, we all need to live in balance. We all need time to rest and recuperate: our bodies, minds, and souls. If you only charge your phone for five minutes, how can you expect it to run for the five hours you need?

Stress can be a good thing because it can help us get things done. It's normal to experience stress because, realistically, nobody lives an unstressed life. But it is not okay to be stressed all the time.

We all need to recharge and take care of ourselves. When you board a flight, you often hear the flight attendant reminding all the passengers that if an oxygen mask drops down in front of you, be sure to put your mask on before helping others. Very much like life, you need to take care of yourself before you take care of others.

You and I know too well what lack of rest does to the body and mind. When I get overburdened and don't get enough sleep, I end up feeling sick, I get easily irritated, and I find it difficult to think straight. The thing is, even if I don't give up, my body will. Stress doesn't just affect you mentally; it also affects you physically. Here is a list of what stress can trigger in you:

- Headaches and tummy aches
- Rashes and hives
- Insomnia
- Chest pain
- Being more prone to anxiety and depression
- A lowered immune system, making you more prone to illnesses
- The release of toxic chemicals in the body to trigger heart attacks, strokes, and high blood pressure
- Accumulation of fat in the body (Oh, that sucks.)
- Increased production of sebum in the skin, triggering more acne (Yikes.)
- Wrinkles (OKAY, DEALBREAKER!!!!!!)

Does this sound familiar? You stay up late, wake up early, and don't let yourself have fun because you're too busy trying to check everything off your to-do list. Sorry to break it to you, but even when all those items get checked off, new ones will simply replace them. There are always more errands and more deadlines to come.

About a year ago, I was having the most stressful day. My husband was out of the country, leaving me alone to juggle our toddler and work for two weeks. The house was an absolute pigsty. There were piles of laundry that needed to be done, and dishes were overflowing from the sink. I had dozens of emails to respond to and several deadlines to meet for my clients.

Since I had been frustrated for the entire day, I even snapped at my toddler when he was getting restless. Desperate, I used the television as a temporary nanny to distract him and went back to my dining table to stress out in front of my laptop. Isaac's favorite show, *Paw Patrol*, came on, but he was not interested. Even though he knew I could yell at him again, he was still eager to tug my hand to lead me somewhere. I took a deep breath to calm down and followed him down the hallway to our front door. Oh no. He wanted to go outside for a walk. And with his tiny little feet, I knew it would take up a fair amount of time.

We had both already bathed, and I just didn't have time for it, but I decided to put our coats on, anyway, and go outside. As we walked around our neighborhood, I stopped to point out the trees and flowers to him and realized just how beautiful our surroundings were. I noticed that the cherry blossom trees had started to bloom. The air was clean and fresh, and the sun was beaming down on us. Usually about halfway through the walk, Isaac would ask me to carry him, but on this day, he walked for most of the journey. After all that, I had Isaac to thank, because that walk was exactly the mental relaxation that I needed. Usually after he goes to sleep, I catch up on my work, but on that night, I relaxed with a book instead. The next day, I was able to focus much better, as I was in a better mood.

A week from now, Isaac will not remember whether I cleaned the house or finished my work; however he will remember that I spent time with him. Why do we work ourselves crazy to live a worrying and stressful life? The purpose of life is not to get everything done, but to enjoy each step along the way. I've mentioned how important it is to listen to others, but it's just as important to listen to yourself. If you find yourself saying "I'm tired" all the time, maybe what you really need is a good sleep. If you catch yourself saying "I'm stressed" all the time, maybe what you really need is to reschedule and rearrange your priorities. If you often complain, "I can't do it alone," then maybe you need to ask for help. You can't do everything at once and even if you tried, you probably wouldn't do a great job at any of it. I cannot stress this enough—nothing is more important than your happiness and well-being.

We tend to think we only deserve rewards when they are given to us by others, but we can do so for ourselves too. I used to have this habit where if I was watching television, I had to do something useful at the same time. It may sound silly to you, but I would feel so guilty about "wasting" my time in front of the TV that I would often mop or dust while I watched to make sure I was making the most out of my time. It was my way of "earning" television time.

It frustrated Tim a lot because even though I would always tell him I wanted to spend more time together, he would often sit by himself on the couch while I motored all over the room with my mop. Even worse, I wouldn't be 100 percent focused on the show, so I'd end up missing important parts and interrupting him to ask what had happened. Even if I wasn't walking around with a mop, I'd catch him rolling his eyes as he looked over at the laptop in my lap.

I had good intentions with all my multitasking; I was trying not to be a lazy or unmotivated person. However, it ended up becoming yet another bad habit because it made me believe succeeding in life meant I had to be productive every minute of the day. When you are distracted all the time, it's impossible to be fully present for others. Life is about being, not doing. *(Or perhaps we would've been called human doings . . .)* Learning to be still has been my biggest challenge of the year. We shouldn't let ourselves become so used to noise and commotion that we don't even know how to sit still anymore. Tim eventually stopped watching television with me unless I promised I could sit undistracted next to him.

"I don't have time to sit still for an hour," I protested, even though I knew it was a big, fat lie.

"You know that you and I have the same number of hours in a day," he argued back. Damn.

"But I have more on my plate than you do," I'd respond, slightly cattily.

"Those commitments are your choice." He knows he is right. I know he is right. Damn, again . . .

I know that if I truly want something done, I will find a way to make sure it gets done. When we say "I don't have time," what we really mean is, "It's not a priority."

For example, saying you don't have time to go to the doctor means that your health is not a priority. Saying you don't have time to catch up with friends means that friendship is not a priority. The fact that I didn't have time to sit and watch TV with my husband meant my husband was not a priority. I needed to get my priorities straightened out so they were in harmony with my happiness and those around me.

One day not long after Tim's little lecture, I agreed to sit next to my husband and watch an episode of *Suits* with zero distraction. At first it felt weird to be sitting on the couch with nothing in my hands or lap. Is this what I'm supposed to do? Just sit here and twiddle my thumbs? But after a while, I was able to settle into the moment and enjoy that quiet time with my husband. Now, a few times a week after our son goes to bed, we make it a routine to watch a little television together before bedtime.

We humans have accidentally conditioned ourselves to need to be constantly stimulated. We are always watching, doing, or listening to something. I've recently started a new habit of embracing quietness. After brushing my teeth and washing my face in the morning, I used to go downstairs and immediately turn on the television as I prepped breakfast. Like many of you, I relied on being distracted to be entertained.

One exceptionally gorgeous morning, something made me decide to eat my breakfast in silence, appreciating the lovely weather outside. Instead of feeling bored, I felt peaceful. I was completely relaxed and able to appreciate the birds chirping outside as the beautiful sunlight streamed through my windows. The silence made me feel as if my senses were heightened, and I was able to enjoy my breakfast even more.

I love listening to the radio when I'm driving, but now often enough, I will drive in complete silence because it allows me to focus on my thoughts. You don't have to go to a spa to feel relaxed; you can simply sit in a quiet room for a few minutes and take some deep breaths. Try it. It may feel a little odd in the beginning, but as you do it more, the feeling of awkwardness will be replaced by a feeling of harmony. Both our bodies and minds deserve a break from our overactive lifestyles. When you allow yourself to take breaks, you will bounce back more focused and sharp. Don't be afraid to let yourself be bored, because it can actually be a good thing. It teaches you to clear your mind and relax.

You Can't Do It All

Anyone who tells you that everything in their life is going perfectly is a LIAR. Even those who look as if they have it all together are definitely losing it on the inside from time to time. Would you believe me that it wasn't until last year that I finally realized that it's just not possible for me to do it all? I ignored the warning signs, and I was oblivious to the simple fact that whenever I'm winning in one area in my life, I am also falling behind in another.

I know now that as I progress in my career, I'll just have more opportunities and responsibilities coming my way. At the same time, as my family continues to grow, they will also demand more of my time. When I'm killing it with my writing, I'm missing out on precious story time with my son. Whenever I'm spending time with my family, I'm missing deadlines and meetings. To maintain balance, sometimes I have to drop something because it's not possible for me to do it all. Yes, there will be some sacrifices and losses along the way, but as long as I keep my highest priorities in balance, I'll be all right.

Not long ago, I was asked by one of my subscribers whether it was even possible to have it all. It was a great question, one that has been asked of many working women who are trying to juggle life's priorities. But there is no answer to that question. Or more accurately, the answer is different for everyone, as it depends on what you define as "having it all." To some, maybe it means being able to live freely and authentically; to others, it might mean being able to stay warm at night with a full belly.

To most people, the concept of having it all means having a loving family, a successful career, a thriving social life, and good health. As a woman, I understand the pressure we get from society to "have it all," which also somehow means if we don't, we're supposed to feel incomplete. Maybe there are some people in the world who do have it all, at least on paper, but I'm fairly certain they don't do it all on their own and that there are many sacrifices along the way. Celebrities can hire nannies and chefs and all the help in the world, but it still must be difficult juggling time between work and family. Nobody can be in two places at once, after all.

I will say it again and again: What's most important is *balance*. Maybe there have been moments when other people have thought that I "have it all," but I can tell you that under my forced smile, I was probably going crazy inside. It's never easy spinning too many plates when you only have two hands.

So in answer to that nice woman's questions—I don't know if it's possible to have it all. I certainly never truly did, because as I tried to juggle all my priorities, I didn't have the peace I needed. Accepting that the concept of "having it all" was in fact a myth was actually a huge sigh of relief for me. I can only focus on doing what I can rather than dwelling on what I cannot. I don't need the best of everything; I just need to make the best out of everything I have. When I have my inner peace, I am less distracted by life's "supposed" demands, so I can focus on doing what truly matters to me. It doesn't matter where I am in life right now. I don't have to have everything figured out for me to celebrate my life. I just need to be able to do what I'm passionate about and believe in my worth. Then, to me, I have it all.

Ready, Set, Relax

Tim and I just got back from a five-day trip with friends in Iceland, and we had an amazing time. I've always wanted to chase the northern lights, and the fact that we managed to catch them while bathing in a warm blue lagoon was an absolute dream come true.

The thing is, vacations can actually end up being more exhausting than anything else, since you're more likely to go out and explore. Nonetheless, vacations are wonderful because you are gaining experience while giving your mind a break from your usual day-to-day life. Even a quick and relaxing day break can recharge you.

But don't think you must go on a vacation in order to de-stress. I used to believe holidays were the magical cure for stress, but as great as the holiday ends up being, you eventually have to return back to reality. Vacations are wonderful for the heart and soul, but they are not the answer to effectively relieving stress in the long run.

There are actually a lot of things you can do to help yourself wind down and find inner peace and relaxation. Surprisingly, the most effective ones are often free or at least low cost. I'm going to share some of my favorite ways to de-stress. We all need to give ourselves time to recharge and relax, so try a few of my suggestions out to see what works for you. Some of you (the workaholics, like myself) may feel uneasy at the beginning. Don't give up too soon, though. Keep at it because unwinding is something you have to teach yourself in order to wean yourself away from constantly feeling the need to be busy.

Exercise Your Way to Happiness

When in doubt, exercise. Getting your heart rate pumping may be the last thing you feel like doing when you're stressed, but it turns out it's one of the most effective remedies. Not only is exercise good for keeping our bodies looking and feeling great, it's scientifically proven to lower stress, depression, and anxiety. When you exercise, your body releases feel-good chemicals known as endorphins, which make you feel more positive. In this case, not only does exercise make your body stronger, but it also strengthens your mind. Since exercise helps you sleep better, this obviously affects your mood for the better too. Whenever I used to get agitated, I would head straight to my gym to release all that built-up tension. Believe me—no spa, massage, or relaxation sanctuary gives me the mental boost that exercise does.

That being said, I have to admit that I am selective when it comes to my workouts. I cannot stand running for twenty minutes, because I just get plain bored. However, I would be more than happy to jump and dance in an aerobic workout for an hour straight, without a second thought. Maybe some of you like to jog while others prefer to swim. It doesn't matter what you do, as long as you get your heart pumping. There are many different types of workouts out there, so find one that suits you best.

If you are tight on cash, don't think you need some sort of expensive monthly gym membership to get your endorphins pumping. There are plenty of fitness videos you can watch online for free to get you moving. Don't tell anyone, but I had a pretty awesome workout yesterday dancing alone with my mop in my kitchen.

If you need more motivation to exercise, find a buddy to join you. My friend recommended that I go buy cute gym gear to kick-start my exercise plans. At the time, I thought she was nuts, but of course it turned out that she was absolutely right. My new workout clothes totally motivated me to want to work out more.

I always believe that a great music playlist can make all the difference to motivate me to exercise. But maybe music isn't your thing. One of my friends recommended an app he likes called "Zombies, Run!" It is actually a game that requires you to physically run away from zombies. He wasn't a fan of running, either, yet this incentive made him do it. Whatever floats your boat. Whatever works for you.

Create Your Sanctuary

This suggestion is my personal favorite stress reliever. I just love soaking away my worries with a nice hot relaxing bath because it benefits both my body and mind. Bath time helps to encourage sleep because it raises body temperature before allowing it to cool down, which induces your body to go into relaxation mode. The trick is to take a bath (or shower, if you're not a fan of the tub) two hours before your bedtime for best results.

Other benefits of taking a hot bath include the relief of cold symptoms and recovering tired muscles. You can even throw in some soothing bath salts; I like to use aromatherapy bath products with calming scents, such as lavender, for total relaxation. To really turn your bathroom into a spa sanctuary, light a few candles and play your favorite relaxing playlist. To turn it up even more, use the time as an excuse to indulge in a nice facial mask and a good book. Total bliss.

Switch Off

This might be hard for some of you, but it's worth a try: Turn your phone off for at least an hour a day. The reason we find it so hard to relax these days is because we're always switched on. Our mobile phones are no longer just used to make phone calls; we can now take pictures, watch movies, play games, browse the web, and do so much more. Since we rely so heavily on these devices, we look at our device's screen more than the actual people in our lives. We are constantly distracted, all day, every day.

As much as I like keeping up with my loved ones on Facebook, often enough I get frustrated by it. There's a lot of negativity online and the thing is, it can rub off on you. Social media makes us focus more on other people's lives rather than ours. Our source of entertainment does not have to be tied to our phones. Use your time to be in the moment, to focus on yourself and your loved ones. You don't have to always take a picture of whatever you're eating. You don't have to record fireworks and live performances because, let me tell you, no recording will ever be as good as seeing it live. Those videos and pictures will most likely just sit in your camera roll for no good reason. I've taught myself to put away my phone one to two hours before my bedtime because it's been proven that the blue light from our devices' screens stimulates the brain, making it more difficult to relax and fall asleep. Instead, I wind down by reading a good book.

Take a Walk

Remember when Isaac taught me that a simple walk around my neighborhood helped bring back my sanity? My toddler managed to drag me from my laptop and insist we go outside, despite the fact I was having one of the most stressful days. But it was exactly what I needed: a mental break. Sometimes we need to physically remove ourselves from our stressful environment, even if it's just for five minutes. Go outside and take long deep breaths of the crisp fresh air. If you're not a fan of exercising, a brisk walk is all it takes to pump happy endorphins into your body for a happier state of mind. Spending time in nature is proven to reduce stress and boost energy levels. When I'm out walking my dogs, I use the opportunity to reboot while listening to my favorite podcasts. I love my alone time.

Immerse Yourself

Painting has always been my sure-win method if I need my attention diverted. With one stroke of my paintbrush, I escape into a different world and my troubles disappear. When I'm deeply absorbed in whatever I'm painting, it's hard to worry about other things.

Whenever I'm feeling especially stressed, I go straight to my kitchen to prep a meal. Nothing is more therapeutic to me than taking my time to cook a nice dinner for my family. There are plenty of other hobbies you can pick up, such as gardening, sewing, drawing, crocheting, writing, and more. It can be anything, as long as it makes you feel calm and centered. My friend's hobby is making candles, yet she doesn't even like lighting them. Candle making just makes her happy, so she makes a bunch whenever she's stressed. I also love to get my rubber gloves on and scrub the toilet. Don't ask me why, because I don't know either. I just know I love it.

Healthy Eating

Okay, I get it. Whenever you're stressed and up to your armpits with work, it does seem easier to just snack on junk food. Of course it's okay to indulge in ice cream, chocolates, and cookies every once in a while. Some even say that chocolate helps you focus better. Here's the thing, though. I only know that when I'm eating like crap, I end up feeling like crap. We were on the road for much of our trip in Iceland, so we had to rely on eating crisps, sweets, and chocolate all day. I felt groggy every single day and couldn't wait to have some veggies in my belly.

Too much sugar not only makes me feel sluggish but also gets me mega cranky. When you deprive your body of nutrients, of course it won't be able to perform the way it should. Remember to eat in moderation to keep your body in balance. Keep your body, mind, and skin hydrated by drinking plenty of water. Bottom line, the better you eat, the better you will feel, physically and mentally. Nuts are proven to reduce cortisol levels to keep your stress at bay. If you're craving sugar, snack on a banana, because it's packed full of potassium to lower your blood pressure. Chamomile and green tea both have proven de-stressing abilities. Remember to eat without distraction so you can savor every bite. Focus on the taste and texture of your food, turn the process of eating into a moment of meditation, and you will find yourself enjoying your meals even more.

Better Your Environment

Even if you are working, know you can enjoy whatever you're doing more by improving your environment. It's said that indoor greenery can boost the mood, ease stress, and purify the air around us. If you can't find time to go outside, bring the outdoors inside with some potted plants. As I'm typing, I've got three mini-cactus plants in front of me, and I'm surprised how therapeutic it feels to look up from my screen every so often and see those little guys standing there.

I also find that I get very easily distracted if my work surface is messy. I know some of you probably work just fine in an untidy environment, but I always feel like a cluttered space creates a cluttered mind. Speaking of cluttering, can I also mention how great it feels to clean out the hidden spaces, like your wardrobe and cupboards? Even if we shut the doors and the mess is out of sight, it will linger in the back of our minds, giving us a little extra mental burden. If you have some free time, go ahead and tackle that messy closet of yours, and you will feel some pressure lift off your shoulders. I usually like to do this while catching up with a new episode of my favorite sitcom. I always feel so alive afterward. Even if it ends up getting messy again a week later, I promise it's worth it.

True Meaning of Success

In almost every panel or interview, I've been asked, "What are your tips on being a successful YouTuber?" My answer is never quite as technical as everybody else, yet bear in mind, I'm fully aware of the professional steps I need to take in my industry. It's just that I know that in order to flourish, you must first know what true success means.

A lot of teenagers rush to create YouTube channels, hoping to become overnight "YouTube sensations." Then they are often disappointed when their channels don't perform the way they expected. The simple reason is because most of them are making videos with the intention of becoming rich and famous. When they get discouraged because they don't have instant success, they give up before giving their channel a proper chance. To them, they have failed already.

To me, a successful YouTube channel is not defined by the number of subscribers or views. I believe if you can help change one person's life for the better, your channel is more than worthwhile. That person you helped could go on to help more people out there, causing a ripple effect.

I have a handful of good friends who don't have millions of subscribers, but that does not stop them from making videos. YouTube is an outlet for them, and it allows them to express their creativity and their ideas. They make videos because they want to better the lives of others and be inspired in the process, so they don't need millions of subscribers to keep them going. Even though YouTube did not end up being a career path for them, and they went on to have normal jobs on the side, they still continue to make videos today purely because it makes them happy. Since they value the experience more than anything else, they are probably much more content than the bigger YouTubers out there. Success shouldn't be defined by other people's standards; it should be defined by you, because only you know what truly makes you happy.

What's the point of earning lots of money if you're living a miserable and meaningless life? I had several YouTube friends that were building up their careers but got lost in depression, all because they were not happy pretending to live the perfect life they were portraying on their social media.

What lifted many of them out of their despair was realizing that the key to success was happiness, rather than the other way round. Like me, when they found a way to live life in balance again by readjusting priorities, things only got better. Some don't earn as much as they did before, but just like me, they certainly feel richer simply because they are now living a much more authentic and meaningful life. Instead of giving in to the pressure of forcing themselves to put out content that others would like to see, they now make content that means something to them. We are no longer burned-out all the time but inspired, instead.

In order to have a successful YouTube channel, you need to be passionate about what you create and share with the world. The very same concept applies for a successful life. You need to know what gives you the most fulfillment and choose to live by aligning yourself to your morals, priorities, and goals. In the end, everything we do in life should be geared toward making ourselves happy.

Most people define success by having a certain social status or having materialistic things, but true success comes in total wholeness. I feel whole whenever I'm joyful, at peace, grateful, appreciated, creative, and serving others. Material gain is only a small aspect of temporary happiness. If I were to look at my success as something that's only achieved through having things, I would always be disappointed, as that would be only a single dimension of success. However, when we are able to do what we love and share our greatest talents and gifts with those around us, we flourish in every direction of our lives. This is multidimensional success—real success.

The Jar of Life

Compassion, love, kindness, and inspiration are all meant to be shared, after all. When we are able to share our gifts with others, it automatically brings us happiness and hence, a successful life.

I want to tell you a story I read that was shared on my Facebook feed years ago. Many of you might already be familiar with it, but I want to retell this story because I love what it teaches us about the philosophy of life:

One day, a teacher placed an empty glass jar in the middle of his desk and filled it with golf balls until he could no longer fit more. He looked at his class and asked if they agreed that the jar was full. Every student nodded and agreed that the jar was indeed full. The teacher then picked up a bag of small pebbles and poured them into the jar of golf balls. The pebbles seeped into the openings between the golf balls and, once again, he asked if the jar was full. Once again, the students nodded and agreed.

The teacher goes on to pick up another bag and, this time, it was filled with sand. Again, he pours it into the jar, and it filled up all the empty spaces left between the golf balls and small pebbles. Again, he asked the class again if the jar was full, and the students agreed. Finally, the teacher took out a cup of coffee from under his desk and poured it into the jar, filling up the empty spaces between the sand. At this point, the students are now laughing and wondering where this is all going.

The teacher waits for the laughter to stop before telling his class, "This jar represents your life. The golf balls represent the important things like your family, children, friends, health, and passions. If everything else was lost and only these remained, your life would still be full. The pebbles represent the other things in life that matter, such as your job, house, and car. The sand is everything else, the small stuff. If you put the sand in first, there would be no room for the pebbles or golf balls. The same goes for life. If you spend all your energy sweating the small stuff, you will never have room for the important stuff. Take care of the golf balls first; the rest is just sand. You are dismissed."

Before the students left, one asked, "You never mentioned what the coffee represents." The teacher smiled and answered, "I'm glad you asked. The coffee just shows you that no matter how full your life may seem, there is always room to have a coffee or two with a friend."

In order to live fully, be serious about setting your priorities, and don't ignore the important things. Because in the end, it's only the important things that truly matter.

Little Joys in Life

Life is not just about the major events and celebratory moments. Most of the time, it's the small pleasures that make us smile each day. Learn to cherish the little beautiful joys in life, because they teach us to enjoy the present moment. The more you become aware of all the beautiful little daily joys, the more pleasant your life will be.

These seemingly fleeting moments actually hold tremendous power to brighten up dull, mundane days. If you are constantly seeking only the big things, you will never be able to appreciate the simple pleasures in life.

Try making a list of all the little joys that make your life truly beautiful and worth living. I'll share a few of mine, and you can add yours in below:

1. Crawling into fresh bedsheets
2. When a stranger smiles at you for no reason
3. Finally being able to pee after holding it for a long time
4. The blissful feeling of total relaxation just before you drift off to sleep
5. Listening to an old song you used to love and reminiscing
6. The smell of freshly cut grass
7. Seeing a fully loaded fridge
8. Waking up naturally before your alarm clock goes off
9. When your favorite YouTuber uploads a new video ;)
10. Jeggings (where have these been all my life?)
11. The sound of crunching autumn leaves under your feet

12. Free samples
13. When the restroom doesn't have a queue
14. When your luggage comes out first at baggage claim
15. The sound of a fizzy drink being poured over ice cubes
16. A continuous run of green lights while driving
17. Laughing so much that your stomach hurts
18. Finding the perfect emoji for a message
19. Free shipping
20. Hearing someone snort from laughing so hard

You can create happiness even from the smallest things in life. What are the little things that make you happy?

_____

_____

_____

_____

_____

Bubz's Rules

- No matter what you choose to do in life, know that time does not wait for you. The beauty of life is that we're not meant to last forever, which should drive us to live each day with meaning and purpose.
- The more you give, the more you receive. When you are able to step outside of yourself to help others, that will give you the most

meaning. True fulfillment comes from being part of something that's bigger than yourself.

- You actually have everything you'll ever need to be joyful. I refuse to be defined by what I have. I would rather be respected as someone who respects others, not as someone who owns nice things. It's possible to work, live, and love without worrying about all the material things. Your sense of self-worth should always be bigger than your bank account.

- Having purpose is when you're able to do what's meaningful to *you*. It comes from knowing what your gift is and being able to share it with the world. A meaningful life is not about being wealthy, popular, or having status; it's about being able to live authentic and grateful lives, knowing what our talents and gifts are while being able to share them with others.

- Stop focusing on other people's journeys and focus on your path. Use your energy to focus on building your character and skills. Your destiny is not to be the same as everyone else. Everyone is meant to walk their paths, so cherish and enjoy your journey.

- Don't wait for the future to be happy because, guess what? You actually don't have control over the future. Happiness can only be now, because it is the only time that truly exists.

- The concept of "having it all" is a myth. Focus on doing what you can rather than dwelling on what you cannot. You don't need the best of everything; you just need to make the best of what you have.

- Success shouldn't be defined by other people's standards; it should be defined by you. Only you know what truly makes you happy.

The Beginning . . .

cannot believe we are here, at the end of this book, already. What a journey this has been. But we are only at the beginning of yours. Why settle for "the end" when, instead, you can have "to be continued" . . . ?

I can only thank you for putting your faith in me by spending your precious time reading this book. I hope I inspired you to look at life with a much more positive perspective. I can genuinely tell you that writing this book has been a total heart cleanse for myself. In hoping to spread happiness, it has already come back to me as more joy for myself.

I spent most of my childhood doubting my abilities. But now I know that everything I was ridiculed and bullied for in my childhood ended up being the very reasons I am here today. I celebrate my uniqueness because it saved me, and I'm so glad I embraced it. I grew up with people constantly telling me I was "too soft" and "naive" and that people would take advantage of me. Because of this, I buried my kindness, so I wouldn't seem weak, and attempted to be tougher. But after being selfish for many years, I couldn't deny that it only brought me sorrow. Being able to give back to others ended up providing me so much more in return. Now I know my kindness is not a hindrance, but my greatest strength.

A long time ago, when I was a teenager working in my parent's restaurant, a regular customer who happened to be a local psychic grabbed me by the arm as I walked past her table. She said she needed to tell me something, then told me that one day, I would go places, and it would be my personality that would take me there. Since I don't believe in psychic readings, I smiled politely and thanked her for her kind words. Almost fifteen years later, I can tell you that being selfish will never make you happy. Having a big heart only opens up even bigger doors. You and I don't need a psychic to tell us that if you want to be a good leader, entrepreneur, manager, or whatever you dream of—you must learn to be a good person first.

Sometimes your dreams and goals don't come screaming at you full force but rather in the form of a gentle whisper. It can be hard to tune in to that voice when our world gets too noisy. We get distracted by all the opinions and judgment from people around us.

Whenever the world tells you no, take a deep breath and listen to your heart instead. Listen for that gentle whisper from within. Understand that people in life are here to guide you, but the one that is truly responsible for your happiness is you. From here on out, remind yourself to be your own best friend. Be encouraging, patient, and kind to others, yes; but be encouraging, patient, and kind to yourself as well.

Live in gratitude and laugh as much as you can. Yes, life can be tricky. We can get hurt and bruised along the way, but what doesn't kill us only makes us stronger. We cannot control what life throws at us, but we can control our attitudes. Be thankful for these challenges, as they are often blessings and opportunities in disguise to help us grow and learn. Even the unpleasant people in our life are here to give us valuable life lessons.

Happiness is a choice.

Nine years ago, I set up my YouTube channel in the hopes of discovering more for myself. The more I let myself be open, raw, and honest, the less my fears had power over me. I'm no longer ashamed of my reflection, inside or out. I celebrate every part of her because she is me. I know my imperfections are the reason I feel truly beautiful in my skin today. In trying to make people around the world feel happier and more beautiful, I also ended up living a happier and more beautiful life. You don't need to create a YouTube channel to live a beautiful life; you just have to start living more by giving more.

I'll say it again—you learn something best when you teach it, so go out there and show the world what love and happiness is all about. Like a boomerang, I promise you that it will come back to you.

Last, remember that the only thing that is truly your own is your identity—your morals, beliefs, values, dreams, aspirations, purpose, and passion. They are uniquely yours. Protect them. A successful and beautiful life comes whenever you are able to live authentically, by doing whatever gives you meaning and purpose.

With a powerful mind, you become a powerful person. With a beautiful heart, you are well on your way to a beautiful life. Be patient with this journey called life. You will have some good days and some not-so-good days. Don't give up. Don't be discouraged. You may not be where you want to be yet, but the good news is, you are no longer where you used to be.

What makes you unstoppable isn't about how successful you are or how much money you have in the bank. What makes you truly unstoppable is when you finally are able to be completely confident and at peace with who you are.

Life is a magnificent journey that blesses us with the opportunity to love, learn, and live each day. When you experience a not-so-great day, find comfort in the fact that the sun will always rise again. Tomorrow is another new day.

You don't have to wait for your life's circumstances to be perfect to be happy. For all you know, you will be waiting forever. Choose to be joyful now, because now is the only moment that truly exists.

Don't miss this moment, because you'll never get it back

When you nurture your heart with kindness and love, you ignite it with power, and it will glow. When you shine and radiate warmth, people will naturally be drawn to you. You will never have to be afraid of darkness, because your inner light will illuminate your path wherever you go.

Now go. You are ready to show the world what you are capable of. Go off and start your journey.

You are capable of greatness. May you love boldly and live courageously.

Love, your friend Lindy
(aka Bubz)

Acknowledgments

Tim, you are my favorite person in the world. Thank you for joining me on this crazy adventure we call life. We grew up together, dreamed together, failed together, and found love again together. Now we are building a future together, and there is nobody in the world I would rather do it all with than you. You sacrificed your own dreams so you could become a part of mine. Even though you and Isaac always got up to no good, you took care of him day in and out so I could finish this book. Thank you for not only being the best husband but also the best father to our two children.

Kenn, you are not only my kickass manager, but you are also a dear friend who has always had my best interests at heart. You had the same vision as I did to build schools for the less fortunate, and I am forever grateful to you, not only because you helped to make it happen, but you even ventured halfway across the world to help paint the classroom walls in Laos. I cannot wait for our next field trip to Ghana this year.

To my StyleHaul family, you believed in me from the very start, even before I did. I am forever grateful for all the blessed opportunities you have given me throughout the years, especially during this book journey.

To the team at Adaptive, thank you so much for helping me bring my dream of writing a book to reality. You have been such wonderful partners in this exciting endeavor, and I couldn't be happier with the final result.

Thank you to everyone there, from Matt and Marshall, who kick-started this dream, supported me throughout the process and made the trains run on time, to Whitney who designed the gorgeous cover and design, to the folks at Neuwirth who did all the fantastic typesetting, and to everyone else there who has done so much work to get this book onto shelves and into people's hands. I feel so lucky to have found such a wonderful partner in this process.

Annie, you are not only my best friend but also my biggest cheerleader. You're like a superhero in disguise, but instead of being dressed in spandex and a cape, you come in joggers and a top-knot bun. While I was scratching my head trying to work on my book, you often popped up at my door unannounced to make sure I remained nourished with food and water and positivity. You have been there for me throughout the highest highs and lowest lows of my life. I will never forget the words you said to me as I got on the train, ready to move to the other side of the world: You said "Go take over the world, Bubzbeauty," and so I believed I could.

Jane, not only do I believe I have the most talented editor, I believe I also made a lifelong friend. Thank you for helping me every step along the way as we crafted this book together.

Last but not least—to my Bubz family: No words can describe just how thankful I am for each and every single one of you. You guys have kept me going all these years and continue to inspire me every day. I feel humbled every time I'm told that my videos have helped to change lives for the better. But honestly, you have no idea just how much I lean on all of you at the same time. This book would most certainly not have happened without your never-ending support. Words just barely break the surface of my feelings for you all, so I plan to continue to say thanks by making you this promise: I promise you all that I will keep working hard to create for you and inspire you as much as you inspire me. From the bottom of my heart, thank you for inviting me into your lives, not just as a beauty Vlogger, but also as a friend and sister.

To the reader of this book, thank you from the bottom of my heart for choosing this book to spend your precious time with. This book is dedicated to you.

May you never forget that you are capable of greatness.

Bubz Bibliography

Some of the articles, books, and studies I reference in the book are as follows:

Binazir, Ali. "Are You a Miracle? On the Probability of Your Being Born." Huffington Post, August 16, 2011. http://www.huffingtonpost.com/dr-ali-binazir/probability-being-born_b_877853.html

Davis, Bruce. "There Are 50,000 Thoughts Standing Between You and Your Partner Every Day!" Huffington Post, July 23, 2013. http://www.huffingtonpost.com/bruce-davis-phd/healthy-relationships_b_3307916.html

Goewey, Don Joseph. "85% of What We Worry About Never Happens." https://donjosephgoewey.com/eighty-five-percent-of-worries-never-happen/

Leahy, Robert L. *The Worry Cure*. New York: Harmony Books, 2005.

Luftman, Debra and Eva Ritvo. *The Beauty Prescription Book*. New York: McGraw-Hill Education, 2008.

Marcus, David K. and Rowland S. Miller. "Sex Differences in Judgments of Physical Attractiveness: A Social Relations Analysis" Personality and Social Psychology Bulletin. 29.3 (2003) 325-335. Print.

Mithen, Steven. "Our 86 Billion Neurons: She Showed It." *New York Review of Books*, November 24, 2016. http://www.nybooks.com/articles/2016/11/24/86-billion-neurons-herculano-houzel/

Sharma, Vijai P. "Positive Emotions Create an 'Upward Spiral.'" *Mind Publications*. http://www.mindpub.com/art399.htm